This annual belongs to...

The PONY ANNUAL 2019

INSIDE YOUR ANNUAL

Published by DJ Murphy (Publishers) Ltd, Marlborough House, Headley Road, Grayshott, Surrey GU26 6LG

Who did what in PONY – The Annual
Contributors Jo Browne, Rachel Dyke, Emma Duncan, Georgia Guerin, Jessica Lewis, Victoria Rea, Bethany Searby
Design Lizzi Porter, Sophie Rigby, Adam Witt

PONY magazine is published every four weeks. To find out more about PONY magazine, visit ponymag.com

Printed by Graphicom via dell'Industria – 36100 Vicenza, Italy

ISBN 978-0-9928279-5-3

Make

Look for the pages with this star and try our fab makes

Olympia HORSE SHOW

Everything you need to know about this super-Christmassy horsey extravaganza

With heaps of exhilarating equestrian action spanning seven days – plus loads of horsey shopping – it's no wonder competitors and spectators alike spend all year looking forward to The London International Horse Show, more commonly known as Olympia. Whether you've never been before or attend every December, here's all you need to know about the spectacular, festive horse show.

DID YOU KNOW?

More than 100 years ago, tickets for Olympia were much sought after. There are reports of some tickets selling for £5, which in today's money is equivalent to £415!

History

Olympia was first held in 1887 – just a year after the venue opened. It was a popular event, but back then the programme of classes was mostly showing and driving. In fact, showjumping wasn't even added to the schedule until 1907 and it was called 'the jumping course'. The competitors tackling the course were mounted officers serving in armies across the globe – there weren't any professional showjumpers like Ben Maher or Jessica Mendoza back then!

One very popular class loved by spectators of the past was the high jump. Much like the Puissance classes of today, riders jumped their horses over a single, slightly sloped fence that was raised in-between each round to see who could clear the highest fence. These days, you won't see the traditional high jump at Olympia, but Nick Skelton set the British record of 2.32m at Olympia in 1978 – and he still holds it today!

What's on

It's not all showjumping, dressage and showing! No matter what day you visit, there's always a totally epic display to look forward to at Olympia. Here are some of the most popular that return year after year.

DID YOU KNOW?
At the first Olympia horse show, the equivalent of £83,000 was spent on flowers alone!

SHETLAND PONY GRAND NATIONAL

Fast, furious and super-funny, you'll see the Shetland Pony Grand National during every evening performance. Eleven ponies and their jockeys speed around the arena, flying over jumps. It's just like horse racing, but in miniature! What's not to love?!

METROPOLITAN POLICE RIDE

If you're a thrillseeker, then look no further! The nail-biting police ride sees mounted officers perform unbelievable stunts, such as jumping through rings of fire or removing their saddles mid-canter, all while in perfect formation. It's awesome!

FREESTYLE TO MUSIC

Get ready for some real-life dancing horses! Freestyle to music is the ultimate dressage competition where riders design their own test to their fave tune! As well as showcasing super-difficult movements, horses must also move in time to the beat.

PUISSANCE

Olympia wouldn't be Olympia without its signature event, the mighty Puissance! It's the ultimate test to see just how high the world's top horses and their riders can jump. The Puissance wall's built from hollow wooden blocks so the slightest touch can knock them down. The starting height is usually around 1.70m, but the wall almost always ends up well over two metres tall.

DID YOU KNOW?
During the Christmas finale, 26 litres of fake snow is used.

DOG AGILITY

Watching horses jump round a course is all well and good, but dog agility at Olympia is mega-fun! These canine superstars fly over obstacles, up ramps and through bending poles at the speed of light. It's great fun for everyone – especially the pooches!

CHRISTMAS FINALE

The evening performance at Olympia can mean only one thing – the Christmas finale. There's singing, dancing and an appearance from Father Christmas himself! It's the perfect way to get into the festive spirit.

Perfect your POSITION!

Want to know exactly what makes a perfect position? Find out here

Having a good riding position isn't just about looking neat – it keeps you secure in the saddle, too. That means, should your pony spook, trip or refuse a fence, you're best-placed to stay on board. It also helps when it comes to giving effective aids, because a perfect position allows you to communicate with your fave pony more effectively.

How your position should look depends on what discipline you're taking part in – a dressage position won't be much help on a cross-country course! But if you break it down into a flatwork and jumping position, you'll soon discover how you sit in the saddle can help you and your pony.

FLATWORK

Hands

These should be positioned just above your pony's withers. Keep your fingers closed around the reins to prevent them slipping, but avoid clamping them tight because this can cause too firm a contact, which could be uncomfortable for your pony.

Feet

Push your weight down through your heels while you're riding, so your heel sits lower than your toe. Avoid jamming your heels down as far as possible, though, as this will cause you to stiffen through your leg and body.

Head

Your head is one of the heaviest parts of your body, so how you hold it really affects your balance. Keep your eyes up, looking in the direction you're riding, and this will help you keep your chin up. Looking down can affect the rest of your position and put you off balance, which will affect how your pony goes, too.

TOP TIP

Keep your hips relaxed because this helps you stay with your pony's movement. If you stiffen up, you'll find it much harder to stay comfy in the saddle.

Body

Think about pulling your shoulders back and slightly down – not up – as this keeps you tall in the saddle. It also opens up your chest, which encourages you to sit evenly across both seatbones, helping you stay straight.

Arms

Keep your arms soft, with a gentle bend in your elbows. There should be an imaginary straight line from your elbow, along your arms and down your pony's reins to the bit. Keeping your elbows bent helps ensure a straight line and makes sure your contact is soft and elastic.

Legs

Your legs should be wrapped around your pony's sides with your heel in line with your hip. This keeps your leg in the correct place to give aids to your pony and keeps you secure should your pony misbehave! So, relax your knees to help you keep your legs wrapped around his sides.

TURN OVER FOR YOUR JUMPING POSITION

JUMPING

Hands
Move your hands forwards along your pony's neck as he jumps the fence. This allows him to stretch through his neck and prevents you catching him in the mouth, which is painful for him and can make him less willing to jump in the future. If you feel unbalanced over the fence, grab hold of a piece of mane or a neckstrap to help keep you secure.

Feet
Push your weight down into your heels and try to keep your toes pointing forwards, rather than sticking out to the side. This helps keep your leg in a strong position at the girth.

Head

Look up and towards the next fence as you jump. Looking up and ahead helps keep your head up, which as well as keeping you in balance in the saddle, also lets your pony know which direction he'll be turning on landing.

> "Look up and towards the next fence as you jump"

TOP TIP
Remember to keep your shoulders back on the approach to the fence, as this helps keep your body upright until you need to get into your jumping position.

Body

When your pony jumps, your body should fold at your hips and lift out of the saddle. Think about bringing your hips back, rather than rising forwards out of the saddle. This keeps you central over the saddle, which will help you to stay balanced.

If you throw your body forwards, it shifts your weight onto your pony's shoulders, which makes it harder for him to jump and more likely that he'll knock a pole.

Legs

Your legs are the most important part of your jumping position! A strong leg position keeps you secure in the saddle and is the key to good balance. Keep your legs wrapped firmly around your pony's sides and soften your knees, because gripping with them causes your lower leg to slide back.

TOP TIP
Have your stirrups at least two holes shorter than your normal flatwork length to help you get the best jumping position.

What's your pony REALLY THINKING?

Do you know why your pony behaves the way he does? Here's what he's really thinking...

Unfortunately, ponies can't talk to us to let us know what they're thinking. But learning to understand his habits and body language can help you read your fave pony's mind!

GIRTHING BOTHER

"Oi – watch it!"

If your pony pulls a face or turns around to nibble you when you do up his girth, it could be that he's feeling a bit uncomfortable. Having something quickly pulled tight around his belly could cause him discomfort, so make sure you do it up gradually to help make it more comfy for him. If he's normally well-behaved and he's suddenly nipping you, he may be trying to tell you that something doesn't feel right, so ask your vet to check him over.

LET'S GO EXPLORING

"Waheyyyy, freedom!"

Taking your pony out for a hack is super-fun. He loves leaving the yard and seeing new places, so can you blame him for getting a bit excited? If he's being particularly fizzy or cheeky, why not ask a friend on a quiet pony to come along, too? Make sure you take it steady until your pony's learned that going for a hack isn't something to get over-excited about.

COMING IN

"Absolutely not! Try again later!"

Your pony is a herd animal, which means he's most happy when he's with his friends in the field, just being a pony. Sometimes, though, this means he'll do whatever it takes to stay with them – including high-tailing it to the other side of the field! It's important not to get fed up and chase him, though, as he'll run away – instead, turn away from him until he gets curious and wanders over. Then, once you've caught him, give him a treat so he learns there's a reward for coming in.

DINNER TIME!

"Hurry up, I'm hungry!"

When it's dinner time on the yard, some cheeky ponies can become very impatient because they want to ensure they get their dinner now! If your pony kicks his stable door, don't be tempted to feed him faster, as this will reward him for his bad habits. Instead, wait until he stops kicking and stands quietly, even if it's just for a few seconds, then feed and praise him.

PAMPER SESH

"Oh, that's the spot!"

When grooming, it's all about the elbow grease. Putting in lots of effort doesn't just make your pony gleam, it's gives him a massage, too, which he'll love. In fact, it can tickle him if you brush too lightly, so don't be afraid to get stuck in! Watch his ears, if they're floppy and relaxed, you'll know he's enjoying himself.

A LITTLE PRAISE

"Treat please – I don't work hard for nothing!"

Pleasing you is always on your fave pony's mind, so after he's been well-behaved, it's important to show him you appreciate it. You could give him an extra scratch, a pat or even a treat. If he learns that being good will be rewarded, then he'll be more likely to behave in the future. Make sure he knows you appreciate his hard work, but be careful about offering too many treats because he could become pushy or nippy.

HOME ALONE

"Yay, finally we can do what we want!"

There's nothing worse than arriving at the yard to find the ponies have caused chaos during the night. With fencing down and rugs ripped, some are always up to no good. If your pony's super-cheeky, it could be because he's getting a bit bored in his field or stable. Make sure he has plenty of forage to keep him busy and you could give him a treat ball or toy to entertain him.

Make UNICORN SURPRISE CUPCAKES

They're super-cute, fun to make and taste yummy, too

To make 24 cupcakes, you'll need...

- mixing bowl
- 24 cupcake cases
- cupcake tins
- a piping bag and nozzle
- four eggs
- 250g caster sugar
- 390g butter
- 250g self-raising flour
- 1 tsp vanilla essence
- 1 tsp baking powder
- 290g icing sugar
- one block of white regal icing
- food colourings of your choice
- decorations of your choice
- sweets – small ones work best

TOP TIP
Why not make these cakes at a unicorn-themed sleep over?

TOP TIP
Try different colours to make the cakes even more magical – they could be pink, purple, blue or even multicoloured!

How to make them

1. Beat 250g of butter and the caster sugar together until light and fluffy, then add the flour to the bowl and mix well. Beat in the eggs, vanilla essence, food colouring and baking powder. Once it's thoroughly combined, place the mixture into the cupcake cases. Bake in the oven at 180°C (gas mark four) for about 20 minutes. They should be springy to the touch and a light golden colour. Transfer them to a wire rack to cool.

Ask an adult for help when using the oven or handling hot cakes and pans.

2. To make the buttercream icing, combine the icing sugar with the remaining butter. Add a few drops of vanilla essence and a food colouring of your choice. Once mixed, place in the fridge to chill until you're ready to use it.

3. While the cakes are cooling, you can start to make the decorations. Take the regal icing and split in half. Add a few drops of food colouring to one half, then knead the icing until the colour is evenly distributed.

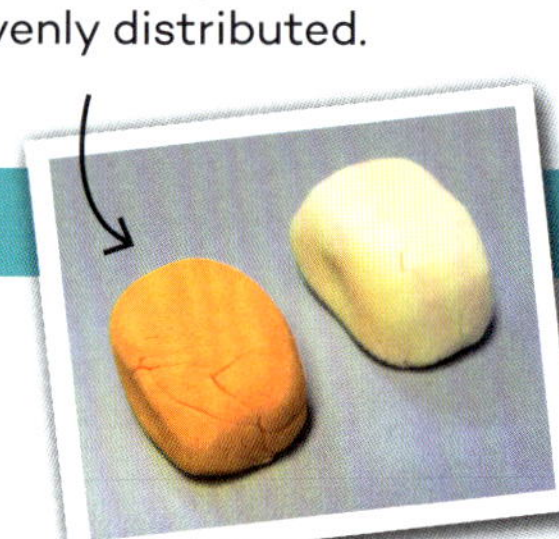

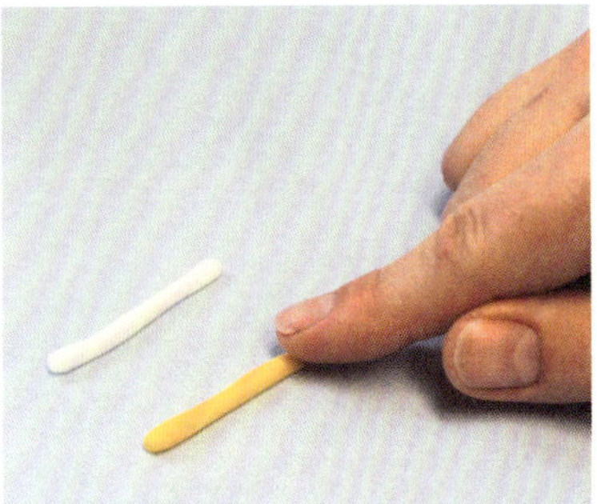

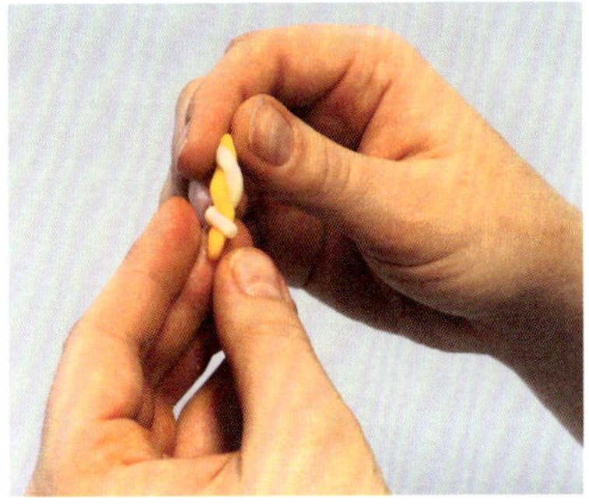

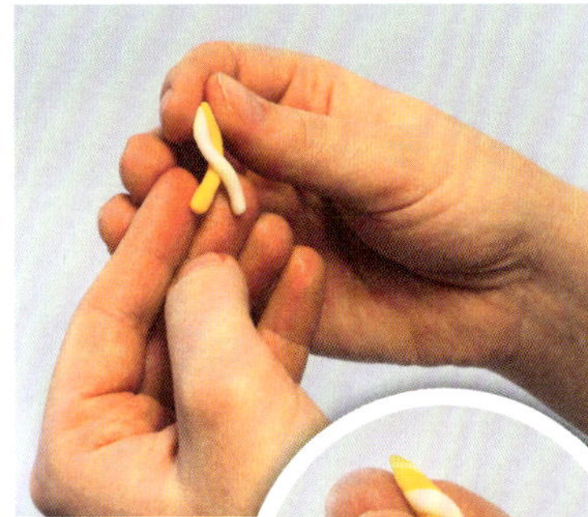

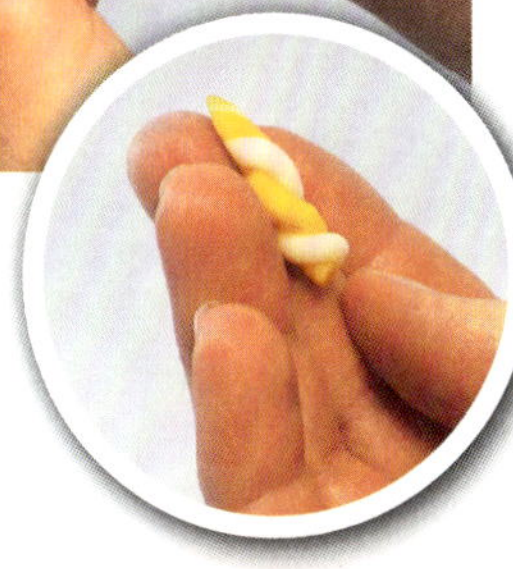

4. Take a small amount of each of the pieces of icing – about the size of a large pea – and gently roll them out into two thin sausage shapes.

5. Place the rolled out icing sausages next to each other, then twist them round each other, pinching one end to form the tip of the unicorn horn. Repeat steps three and four until you have one unicorn horn per cupcake.

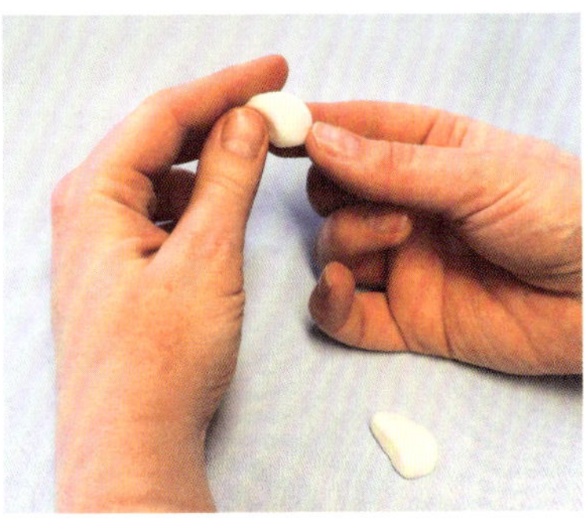

Always ask an adult for help when using a knife.

6. To make the ears, take the uncoloured icing and make two balls of equal size – they should each be roughly the size of a small marble.

7. Take one of the balls and, using your thumb and index finger, mould the icing into the shape of a small pony ear. Repeat until you have two ears per cupcake.

8. Once the cakes are completely cool, use a knife to cut a small circle in the top of them. Remove the top, and cut off any excess until just a small disc remains. Fill the cupcake with sweets, then place the disc back on the cake. Repeat until all the cakes are filled.

TOP TIP

You can use the icing nozzle instead of a knife to cut a disc from the cake. Press the wide edge of the nozzle into the cupcake and twist it a few times, then lift it out. Trim away the excess cake.

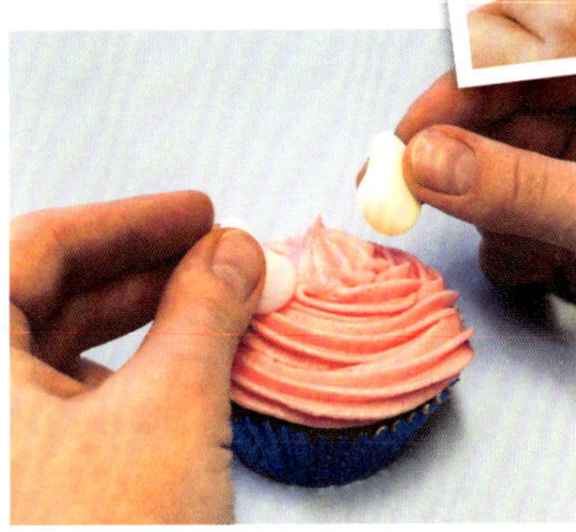

9. Remove the buttercream from the fridge and spoon into the piping bag. Swirl the icing onto the cake in a spiral, finishing with a peak in the centre.

10. Place a horn in the centre of the cake with an ear on either side, pressing them firmly in place. Then add your choice of decoration – you could even use edible glitter to add a bit of sparkle!

Ta-dah!

Super SHETLAND PONIES

DID YOU KNOW?
A Shetland pony, LCpl Cruachan IV, is the official mascot of The Royal Regiment of Scotland.

Easily recognisable, Shetland ponies are known for their small size, big personalities and even bigger mop of mane! They're a firm favourite as a riding pony for children and can turn their hoof to almost anything.

Shetlands in action

This versatile breed is commonly used for riding and driving, and can often be seen in the show ring, too. Approximately 2,000 foals are registered with the Shetland pony stud book each year, with official sales attracting buyers from around the world.

The kind nature of Shetlands means they're ideal first ponies, so you're likely to see them at Pony Club events and riding schools. They're courageous and adventurous, meaning they take part in many disciplines from mounted games to dressage and jumping.

Shetlands are also the stars of the popular Shetland Pony Grand National. Qualifiers are held at large shows across the country, where ponies and riders compete for the chance to take part in the finals held at Olympia London International Horse Show.

Native BREEDS

Natural habitat

If you visit the Sheltand Isles, you'll find loads of ponies grazing the hills known as Scattland. Although they may look wild, the ponies are all owned and looked after by islanders known as crofters. The harsh winters on the island often mean the ponies have little grass, so they eat seaweed to supplement their diet.

It was long believed that Shetland ponies were small due to the hard environment of the Shetland Isles, and this belief was only disproved once the ponies who left the island didn't grow any bigger with more food and kinder weather!

DID YOU KNOW?
Shetlands were the first native breed to have a stud book to track their breeding.

Fact file

Height: No bigger than 10.2hh – any ponies under 8.2hh are known as miniature Shetlands
Colour: Any colour except spotted
Place or origin: The Shetland Islands, Scotland
Known for: Their small size, strength, fluffy coat and cheeky personality

Early days

Shetland ponies are known to have lived on the Shetland Isles for more than 2,000 years. The ponies' ancestors are thought to have come to Scotland from southern Europe during the Ice Age, using the ice fields to travel. They were later bred with a pony brought over by the islanders.

DID YOU KNOW?
In the past, fishermen on the islands would use the hair from Shetlands' tails to make fishing lines.

Popularity grows

The ponies have been an important part of island life and were used to help farm the land. In the 1840s, new laws meant that children couldn't work in coal mines and the Shetland pony was the perfect replacement. Their small size and strength made them ideal for pulling carts of coal through the tunnels.

Due to their popularity as a pit pony, loads of Shetlands were sent to the mainland, threatening the future purity of the breed. So, in 1890, the Shetland Pony Stud book was started.

DID YOU KNOW?
The pairs of cones the carriage has to drive through are called hazards.

HORSE SPORTS

SCURRY DRIVING

Scurry driving is all about precision, accuracy and a whole load of speed!

If you've ever been to HOYS or a big county show, you're bound to have seen a pair of ponies zooming round a course while pulling a little carriage. This super-speedy sport's called scurry driving and it's mega-exciting to watch, but what's it all about? Here's what you need to know...

What is it?

The aim of scurry driving is to navigate a course, which takes a team of two ponies, a small scurry carriage and two people – the driver and groom – through a set pattern of 12–14 pairs of cones. The cones have a narrow gap between them, through which the carriage is driven. The twisty course must be completed as quickly as possible, and the team that finishes with the most cones in place and the fastest time wins.

Pocket rockets

Scurry driving can't happen without a pair of pint-sized ponies to pull the carriage – and they've got to be fast! There are two height classes in scurry driving – smalls for 12hh and under, and larges for 12.1–14.1hh.

One of the most popular breeds in scurry driving is the Welsh Mountain because they're speedy, agile, clever and super-cute, but you'll find loads of different breeds at a scurry competition, including Dartmoors, New Forests and Shetlands.

Different sized ponies have different advantages in scurry driving. Welsh Mountain ponies tend to be smaller and can perform tight turns very quickly, but longer-legged ponies, such as New Forests, can cover the ground much faster in straight lines.

A tight squeeze

Galloping between cones sounds easy, right? Well, the scurry carriages have to have a minimum width of 130cm between the two front wheels, and the space between the cones are 170cm, which leaves a gap of only 20cm each side of the carriage. That's shorter than a long ruler!

What's more, on top of each cone is a ball and knocking one off adds four seconds to the team's overall time. This means the driver and groom have to be very accurate when they guide the ponies and carriage through the hazards.

PENALTIES

Dislodging a ball Four penalties
Driver leaving the vehicle 20 penalties
Groom leaving the vehicle First time eight penalties, second time elimination
Passing through a hazard in the wrong direction Elimination
Passing through a hazard in the wrong order Elimination

DID YOU KNOW?

In scurry driving, if the driver drops their whip, the team are eliminated.

Perfect pairs

The pony pairs in scurry driving often have fun or famous pair names, like Salt and Pepper or Wallace and Gromit.

Dynamic duo

So what do the driver and groom do? As you might have guessed, it's the driver's job to guide the ponies through the course, while the groom's role is to sit behind the driver and balance the carriage by leaning in the same direction as the driver asks the ponies to turn. They have to lean right over the edge of the carriage, so it's definitely not for the faint hearted – adrenaline junkies only!

Stolen!

A terrible crime has left Wintermarsh Stables reeling. Can Amisha solve the case?

It was Wintermarsh Stables' turn to host a competition for the local inter-yard show series and Amisha and her best friend, Jody, had entered the pairs jumping class on their fave ponies, Frizzle and Flame. They were the perfect pair – Frizzle was jet black and Flame as white as a dove, not chestnut as his name suggested.

Jody tackled the course first and flew round with Flame. The girls passed their baton perfectly as they'd been practising for weeks.

"Time to go, Frizzle," Amisha whispered as she kicked him on. Keeping her eye on the clock, Amisha guided Frizzle round the twists and turns of the course, jumping each fence perfectly.

They landed after the final fence half a second inside the time to beat, winning the class! The girls rode side-by-side for their lap of honour, beaming. "You were fantastic!" cried Amisha. "So were you," Jody replied, with a grin. The girls agreed to spend the following day at the yard, pampering the ponies as a reward for their hard work.

Something's wrong

The next day, Amisha arrived at the yard early and was shocked to see Jody sat in the office in floods of tears.

"Jody, whatever's the matter?" cried Amisha, rushing over to comfort her friend. "They're gone!" spluttered Jody between sobs, "Frizzle and Flame have been stolen!"

Amisha felt numb and her legs were like jelly. Could it really be true?

Questions, questions

The police were called and an officer from the local force soon pulled up at the yard. "How do you do?" he asked as he came into the office. "PC Bodkins, I..." but before he could get another word out, Amisha stammered: "The ponies, have you found the ponies?"

PC Bodkins didn't know much about the theft. The yard's CCTV cameras had malfunctioned, so they hadn't captured any footage. Ponies had been stolen from other yards in the last few months, but the police didn't think the thefts were linked, especially as one of the previously stolen ponies had been found dumped on the roadside.

"Rest assured, we'll do all we can to find them," said PC Bodkins as he left, "I'll keep you all updated."

Watching and waiting

The weeks that followed were torture for Amisha and Jody. They were heartbroken that they wouldn't be able to ride their ponies in the final inter-yard show at Brook House Farm.

Instead, they busied themselves with helping Diane, the show series' organiser. She'd been reluctant to let them help at first in case they got in the way, but in the end decided it would be good experience for them both.

They helped her put together the class schedules, ordered rosettes, and carried out security and health and safety checks at Brook House, which took their minds off the missing ponies.

"What would I do without you?" said Diane, offering the girls the chance to present the prizes. They exchanged satisfied glances – it was nice to have something to look forward to!

Sudden realisation

The day of the show came, and the girls were so busy that they almost forgot that the ponies were missing every so often. Everything ran smoothly and the pairs class was especially exciting.

As Amisha handed the winners, who were riding two really cute piebald ponies, their rosettes, she thought, 'A month ago, this was us. Now Frizzle and Flame are gone'.

Then she had an idea. She raced out of the ring, grabbed Jody's hand and dragged her to the hay barn. "What's going on, Am?" she cried. "It fits, Jody,

it all fits!" Amisha replied, "Frizzle and Flame were taken the day after they won the pairs class. The other robbery PC Bodkins told us about? That was Blue and Magnum from The Grange..." Amisha paused. "The day after they won the first inter-yard pairs class!" Jody cut in. "Exactly," replied Amisha, "but what if there's a pattern? What if the piebald ponies are now at risk?" Jody was cautious. "I'm not sure, Am," she replied. "What about the pony who was taken from Diane's yard, Huntsman's Retreat? There's no connection there."

Amisha shook her head and looked away: "I hate to say it, Jody, but I have a theory about Diane."

Sheer disbelief

"Think about it," Amisha said, "the pony from Diane's was stolen before their show and turned up again a week later. What if whoever took our ponies did that as a cover up?" Jody looked thoughtful, "Maybe so, but no one was even caught on camera!" Amisha thought for a moment. "But Jody, remember when we did all the security checks at Brook House? Diane asked us to find all the cameras and she had a key to the office. She did this on all the yards holding the show series. If anyone was going to pull off the perfect crime, surely it's *got* to be Diane!"

The girls wanted to tell someone their theory, but were worried no one would believe them, and PC Bodkins didn't even seem interested in the case!

"There's only one thing for it," said Amisha, "we're going to have to catch her in the act tonight!"

> *Silently, they parked their bikes and turned out the lights*

Stakeout

Amisha felt awful for sneaking out of her room so late at night, but catching the pony thief was too important. She slipped out of the house, switched her bike lights on and cycled down the lane to meet Jody.

They soon arrived at Brook House. Silently, they parked their bikes, turned out the lights and crept towards the yard through the back gate – walking right into PC Bodkins! "What're you doing here?" Amisha gasped. "Likewise," he retorted, crossly.

Amelia told PC Bodkins everything and, as it turned out, he'd come to exactly the same conclusion.

"I'm impressed with your detective work," said PC Bodkins, "but you shouldn't have come. Why didn't you speak to an adult?" Amisha pleaded: "We were worried that no one would believe us!" PC Bodkins sighed. "Be that as it may," he said, "it's not safe to be out on your own without your parents knowing. I have another officer stationed here, so I'll drive you both home, and you'll have some serious explaining to do!

Caught in the act

As PC Bodkins drove the girls down the long driveway of Brook House Farm, they spotted a car with the headlights out travelling speedily towards them. PC Bodkins slammed on the brakes and, thankfully, both cars managed to stop in time. "You two stay in the car," said PC Bodkins, "I'll deal with this." The girls watched as the car door opened – and out stepped Diane! Amisha had been right all along.

Diane eventually admitted to stealing the prize-winning ponies. As it turned out, Huntsman's Retreat was in huge debt, and she'd taken the ponies to sell them and take the money. Luckily, she'd been so busy organising the shows and planning the kidnappings that she hadn't managed to sell them yet. All the ponies were returned to their rightful owners – Amisha and Jody were delighted to have their fave ponies back. Life returned to normal, although Amisha got a reputation as the yard detective and was occasionally asked to investigate missing brushes, boots and lunchboxes!

QUIZ

CAN YOU COMPLETE THE COURSE?

Take the quiz to navigate this tricky cross-country course

START

You're in the start box ready to go and your pony starts getting excited. Is it okay to walk him in and out the front of the start box to calm him down?

No → Your first fence is a simple log. Which side should the red flag be on?

Yes → Oh dear! That's not allowed, but luckily the organiser let's you start again, so carry on this time.

Right

Left → Wrong way but luckily no one saw you – kick on!

You're approaching the next fence and your pony's getting faster with every stride. What do you do?

Let him at it – you need to make up time! → Rider error. Go back and try again.

Half-halt to steady him up

There's a skinny fence ahead. How much have you been practising these?

A bit

Loads

Alternative

Direct

You've made it to a combination that other competitors have found quite tricky. Do you take the direct or alternative route?

Great job!

Keep calm, reattempt and carry on

Your pony refuses! How do you react?

Yes

You're approaching the steps. Should you slip your reins as you go up?

Get really cross at yourself then try again

No

Slip them on the way down next time, but carry on!

You've hit a long galloping stretch and your pony's feeling good. Do you go into the two-point position?

Yes

The alternative route takes you through a wooded area and your pony has to adjust to the light. Do you keep your leg on?

Yes

Up and ahead

No

No

As you approach the ditch, where should you be looking?

In the ditch to check how deep it is

You've ended up in the ditch and are eliminated – start again!

Cross the bridges to continue the course!

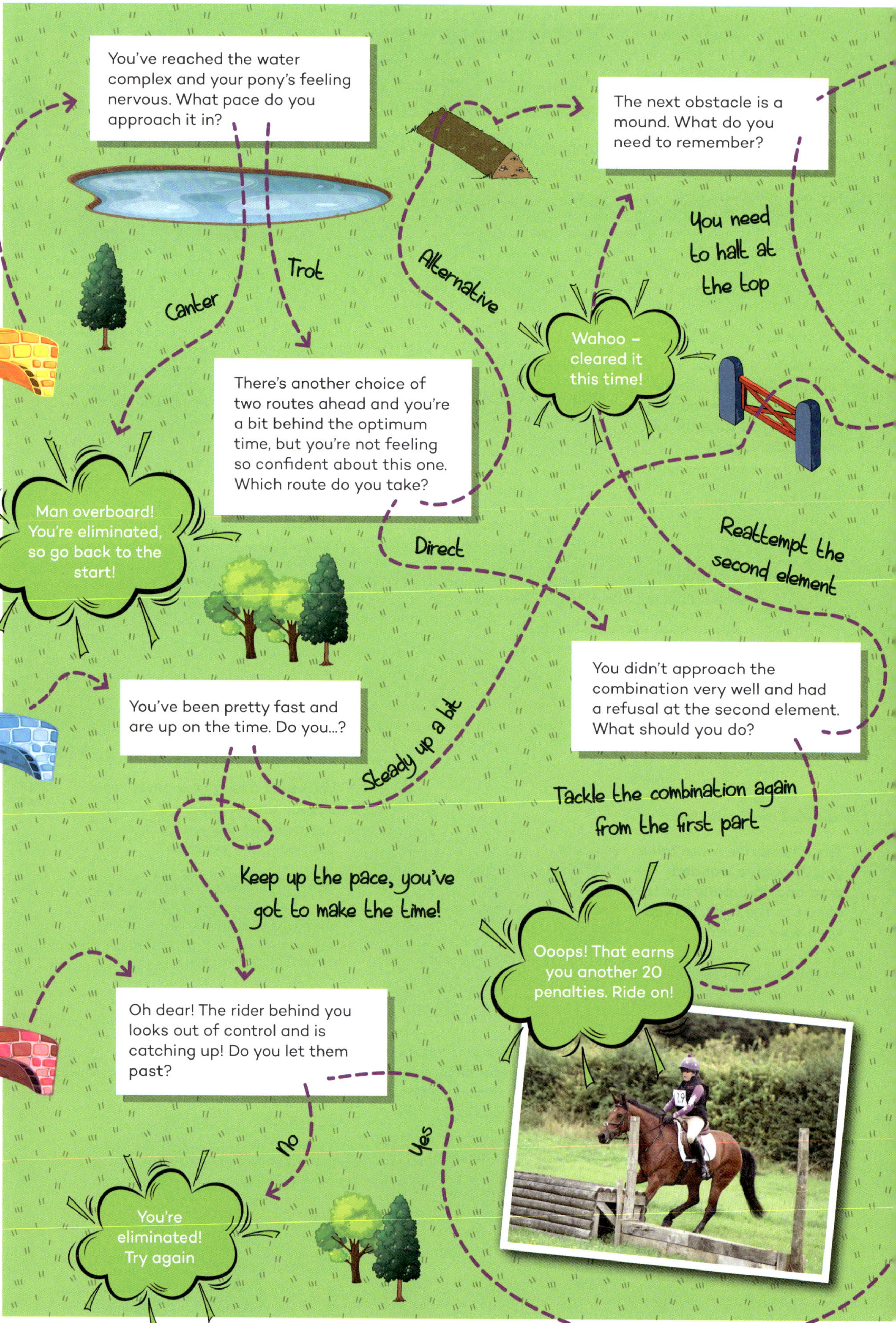
You've reached the water complex and your pony's feeling nervous. What pace do you approach it in?
Canter
Trot
Man overboard! You're eliminated, so go back to the start!
There's another choice of two routes ahead and you're a bit behind the optimum time, but you're not feeling so confident about this one. Which route do you take?
Alternative
Direct
Wahoo – cleared it this time!
The next obstacle is a mound. What do you need to remember?
You need to halt at the top
You didn't approach the combination very well and had a refusal at the second element. What should you do?
Reattempt the second element
Tackle the combination again from the first part
Ooops! That earns you another 20 penalties. Ride on!
You've been pretty fast and are up on the time. Do you...?
Steady up a bit
Keep up the pace, you've got to make the time!
Oh dear! The rider behind you looks out of control and is catching up! Do you let them past?
No
Yes
You're eliminated! Try again
19

To go through both sets of flags

You can see the finish ahead and there's only one more fence to go. What should you avoid?

Relaxing, you're not quite done yet!

Forgetting to smile for the photographer

Twit twoo! You're at the owl hole. Do you...?

Ride as normal and keep your leg on

Duck to avoid hitting any branches

Short and bouncy

What sort of canter should you be approaching the sunken road with?

Long and flat

GREAT ROUND!

Wahoo! That was a fab round! It's hard to make the right decision at such speed but it looks like you've got this under control. You might have found it easy, but don't get too relaxed because anything can happen on the XC course.

ALMOST THERE

Good effort! There may have been a few hiccups along the way, but you got there in the end. Nailing cross-country can only be done with practice, so get out there, work hard and have fun!

BETTER LUCK NEXT TIME

Phew! You've finally made it home, but with a few penalties and you're outside the time. Don't worry, though, because there's loads of time to learn. Turn your mistakes into positives, practise hard and you'll be galloping round clear in no time!

Making mischief

When the humans are away, the ponies will play...

Ruby as Kira
Lucy as Ella
Lily as Daisy
Gem as Tess
Right, Tess and Daisy, I'm going on holiday tonight, so Ella's coming to look after you.
Be good, okay?
They're in their stables ready for you tomorrow, Ella. Thank you so much!
No worries. We'll have a great time.
THE NEXT DAY...
Almost there...
Come on, you try one!
You're right, this is fun!

Right, let's scarper before Ella gets here.
Let's keep her busy then.
Yeah good idea, I can't be bothered to go for a ride today.
That's not enough, watch this!
Be free, ponies!
What on earth's gone on here?!
I think I know who did this...

We can give her a bit of tidying to do.
Right, let's go back to our stables quickly, I'll shut you in.
Those cheeky ponies!
I'm putting clips on your doors when you come in tonight!
You know how to undo the clips right, Tess?
Of course I do!
The end

Cool CONNEMARAS

Native BREEDS

These Irish ponies with really gentle temperaments make perfect all-rounders

Connemara ponies are hugely popular throughout the world. They can regularly be seen dazzling judges in the show ring or showcasing their skills as an ideal all-rounder at Pony Club.

DID YOU KNOW?
A part-bred Connemara named Stroller is the only pony to have competed at the Olympics! He and his rider, Marion Coakes, won a silver medal in the 1968 games for Team GB.

DID YOU KNOW?
The PONY ponies, Duggie and Soloman, are Connemaras.

Where are they now?

Connemaras are famed for their great temperament, strength, stamina and surefootedness, which makes them great ponies for endurance or eventing. Due to their kind personalities, they also make great all-rounders and can often be seen strutting their stuff in dressage, jumping and showing arenas or trying out something new at Pony Club.

Connemara ponies have travelled the globe, and are now a very popular breed in America, Germany and Australia. Although Connemaras are small, cross breeds are well sought after as top-level competition horses.

Liberty rider Emma Massingale works with a team of Connemaras. She rides them without any tack and has taught them to perform a number of other skills, such as letting her stand on their backs and picking things up with their mouths.

Putting on a show

Every year there's a Connemara pony show and festival in Clifden, Ireland, and more than 300 Connemaras are brought to compete. The show includes working hunter classes designed to show the versatility of the breed, mare and foal classes, and a puissance!

The stuff of myth and legend

The origins of the Connemara pony are shrouded in myth and legend. The original ponies were introduced to Ireland by the Vikings, and were used to pull chariots and carts along the beaches. However, a new bloodline was introduced to the ponies in 1588 when the unsuccessful Spanish Armada ran aground in Galway. Legend says the Spanish horses on board the ships swam to shore and bred with the ponies creating the Connemara ponies we know today.

Fact file

Height: 12.2–14.2hh
Colour: They're usually grey or dun, but can be brown, bay, chestnut, palomino or roan
Place of Origin: Connemara on the west coast of Ireland
Known for: Their intelligence, endurance and good temperament

Member of the family

The ponies were important to the local people living near the Connemara mountains, as they were used to pull ploughs and carry baskets full of seaweed, rocks and turf across the rocky terrain.

Families could only afford to keep one pony, and they had to catch and tame a wild Connemara from the mountains themselves. They often chose mares so they could breed them and make money selling their foals. The ponies had to be real all-rounders and have a good temperament because they were also used to drive their families to church on Sundays.

DID YOU KNOW?

The Connemara Breeders Society was set up in 1923 to help preserve and improve the breed.

Pony tales

With the help of her pony, Jacob, Emma reveals exactly what it takes to look after a field-kept pony throughout the year

It's every young rider's dream to own their own pony – just think of the endless cuddles and fun hacks in the sun. But do you really know what it's like to look after a pony all year round? Emma reveals all in her diary...

SPRING

Wahoo! The weather's finally getting warmer even though it's still a bit showery. Jacob's summer coat's on its way, so it's a good time to de-fluff him – it's never-ending!

One thing Jacob's less excited about is his spring diet. He's been doing quite a bit of work over the winter, so he's in pretty good shape at the moment, but now the grass is getting greener, it'll be a lot harder to keep him in good condition.

Although he's never had laminitis before, it's a big worry and I still have to be very careful because any pony can be affected, especially now the field is full of new grass. Plus, Jacob's so greedy that he doesn't know when to stop! I spent ages setting up electric fencing so I can strip-graze him – hopefully he'll stay on the right side!

It's time to start making the most of the longer days and I've managed to get some rides in after school – we've already been on a few short hacks, too. Hacking's great for keeping Jacob fit as well as allowing us to explore loads of cool new routes.

TOP TIP

If you poo-pick every day, it'll be a lot easier to keep your pony's field clear.

SPRING: Remember to...

- ✓ weightape Jacob weekly
- ✓ move the electric fencing
- ✓ check Mum's not giving him extra treats!

Exploring new hacking routes

SUMMER

Yay, here comes the sun – well, at least I hope so! Summer's my fave season because the days are soooo long, plus I can spend all day at the yard in the holidays – no more being told off for daydreaming at school!

Jacob and I are ready for the competition season. We've been practising some showjumping and cross-country, plus we have a few Pony Club rallies in the diary, too. Jacob's been going really well so far and it's nice to see that all our hard work over the winter is starting to pay off – I just need to get him looking the part now!

Jacob loves being in the sun, but isn't so keen on the pesky flies. He always wears a fly mask during the day, which keeps him happy. The grass isn't as lush anymore, so he's got access to his whole paddock and he loves chilling in the shade.

> "It's time to start making the most of the longer days"

SUMMER: Remember to...

- ✓ organise a picnic hack with my friends
- ✓ enter the local fun show
- ✓ pack everything for camp

Time for a quick clip

TOP TIP
Wear a waterproof jacket and trousers when you clip your pony or all his hair will stick to your clothes – I never learn!

AUTUMN

I had such a fun summer and Jacob was on top form! Luckily, the competition season isn't quite over, so I'm looking forward to doing a couple of hunter trials with my friends.

Now that the trees are starting to change colour, pretty woodland hacking routes are my fave. It's also a great time to take Jacob to the beach, as it's much emptier than in summer. Long canters on the beach are a great way to maintain his fitness after a busy summer and it's so much fun!

I've just had a big clear-out and sorted through all Jacob's winter kit. He doesn't need to wear a rug yet, but I want to be prepared, so I've got his rugs ready incase it gets chilly at night.

Jacob's thick winter coat has started to come through and I can't wait to clip him. The clippers have been serviced and Jacob's had a bath so he's clean and ready for a hair cut, I just need to get Mum to help me!

AUTUMN: Remember to...

- ✓ send clipper blades to be sharpened
- ✓ enter a hunter trial
- ✓ organise a beach ride with my friends

> We've taken the opportunity to focus on getting our schooling up to scratch

WINTER: Remember to...

- ✓ check the water trough for ice
- ✓ book a flatwork lesson
- ✓ fence off super-muddy areas of the field

DID YOU KNOW?
Wet, muddy conditions can cause a skin infection called mud fever. Check your pony's heels for scabs, which could be a sign of infection.

WINTER

Winter is, without a doubt, the hardest part of the year. It always seems to be freezing and raining, the fields get muddy and the yard gets icy. This season seems to last forever and the shorter days mean I can't ride as often after school.

Mum's told me there's a chance of snow so, although Jacob lives out all year round, I've got his stable ready just in case the weather gets really bad and his has to come in.

There's less grass in the field at the moment, too, so Jacob's been enjoying a large haynet to make sure he's got plenty to eat – I've not been loving hay getting stuck to my clothes, though!

With the ground being so wet, we've taken the opportunity to focus on getting our schooling up to scratch. There are a few Christmas-themed Pony Club rallies to go to and we've got some dressage competitions booked in to help us keep improving, so we're ready to go again once the competition season arrives in the spring.

Everyday PONY PROBS

Some days at the yard just don't quite go to plan. Here are some scenarios we can all relate to!

KEEPING IT CLEAN

When you're riding with a friend and they notice you've not cleaned your tack in a while.

CHORES, CHORES, CHORES

When your yard owner asks you to do something you've already done, just as you're about to leave the yard.

LET'S JUMP

When your friend raises the jump way too high, but you don't want to say anything.

CATCH ME IF YOU CAN

When your pony refuses to be caught and you have to try not to get cross with him.

GREEDY PONIES

When you're trying to lead your pony to the field but he's got other ideas.

FLATWORK PROS

When you're trying to ride through your next dressage test, but your pony won't concentrate.

Revenge of the riding school ponies

Topper has a plan to teach Lottie a lesson she'll never forget

We were all fed up, so I'd called an emergency meeting with Mitzy, Cosmo and Alfie. We needed to discuss what to do about Lottie. At this time on a Friday we'd usually be fast asleep, resting up for the lessons in the morning, but that evening we were deep in conversation, trying to decide what to do about our least favourite rider.

"Topper, she's a complete menace!" snorted Alfie. "She never listens to Becky's instructions, and kicks our sides and jabs us in the mouth."

"I know, we're all tired of being treated badly by that horrid girl," I agreed, "but I have a plan, listen." The others pricked their ears and huddled closer together in the field. "I heard Becky say tomorrow is a jumping lesson. Becky always pairs Lottie and me together for jumping, so I'm going to teach her a lesson she'll never forget! We'll show her what it's like to have a misbehaving pony."

After I finished explaining my plan, everybody neighed in agreement and we settled down for the night, feeling excited about putting our plan into action tomorrow.

Ready to go

"Are you all ready?" I whispered, as I saw the first group enter the yard. The other ponies nodded eagerly as we listened to Becky assign the riders to their ponies for the day.

"Right, we're going to be doing some showjumping practice today. Lottie, you're riding Topper, Eliza, you're on Mitzy, Kelly's on Alfie and Sarah's on Cosmo. They're all tacked up and ready to go, I'll see you in the arena in five mins." The girls ran excitedly onto the yard to collect the ponies.

"I can't believe you got Mitzy," Lottie sneered at Eliza. "She's the worst pony on the yard. She always knocks a pole." I could see Mitzy swishing her tail angrily and I snorted at her in warning. "I think she's wonderful," Eliza replied stroking Mitzy's neck, "I'm always glad when I get to ride her."

We all waited patiently for the girls to mount, then headed over to the arena where Becky was waiting to start the lesson.

The plan in action

"Okay, let's get started," called Becky. "Kelly, you're lead file for our warm-up today. The rest of you, follow on behind."

"Here we go – remember to be on your best behaviour!" I reminded the other ponies as they trotted past. Lottie and I followed on at the end of the ride and began trotting around the arena. As soon as I felt Lottie's sharp kick, I stopped and started to move backwards.

"Topper! What are you playing at?" Lottie growled angrily giving me another sharp kick. "We're supposed to be going forward!" I kept moving backwards until Lottie stopped kicking me and slumped in the saddle.

> "Topper! What are you playing at?"

"Come on, Lottie, what are you doing? Get Topper warmed up," Becky instructed. "I can't, he won't mooove!" whined Lottie, throwing the reins down on my neck. It was the moment I'd been waiting for. I immediately walked forwards, slotting in behind the other ponies. Lottie scrambled for the reins, quietly muttering to herself about horrid ponies.

"Brilliant, Tops!" chuckled Cosmo as we started to trot round the arena. Every time Lottie gave me a kick that was too hard or jabbed me in the mouth, I did the opposite of what she wanted, while the other ponies were foot-perfect for their riders. I could feel Lottie becoming angrier every time I did something naughty and Becky was keeping a close eye on us.

After we'd all warmed up on the flat, Becky set up a small cross-pole. "Alright everyone, pop over this fence one at a time," she instructed. "Lottie, you and Topper are up first. I want you to focus on your position, push your weight down into your heels, and look up and over the fence." Lottie nodded and began to gather up my reins. As we approached the fence, she started to kick me really hard every stride and, just before I needed to take off, she used her stick to give me a sharp smack on my shoulder. I stopped in front of the fence, and felt Lottie lose her balance and fall onto my neck.

"You stupid pony!" she snarled, giving me another smack with her whip. "Why can't you do as you're told?!" I stood there quietly, as I watched Becky storm over towards us. "Lottie! I won't have anyone treat my ponies like this. They work extremely hard and deserve to be treated with respect," she sounded furious. "Give Topper a pat and line up with the rest of the ride. Once you've calmed down you can try again."

I could hear Lottie sniffling as she leant forwards to give me a pat. The other ponies were stood with their ears pricked and a satisfied expression while their riders all looked a little shocked – it was very rare to see Becky get angry.

Further to go

Lottie was quiet for the rest of the lesson and her riding had become a lot kinder. I was feeling smug that I'd managed to teach her a lesson so easily. The other ponies had thoroughly enjoyed watching Lottie get told off and were still behaving well.

For the final part of the lesson, Becky had built a short course for us to complete as a mini competition, where we'd be judged on style as well as a clear round. Mitzy, Cosmo and Alfie went first and had all gone clear. Lottie and I were the last to go. I was feeling excited as we headed towards the first fence, and Lottie was being a lot more thoughtful and considerate with her riding.

We'd cleared the first three fences with ease and had two more to go. I got the striding slightly wrong on the second to last fence and the pole rattled. As soon as we'd landed I felt a sharp kick and slap of the whip on my shoulder again.

"Pick up your feet, you stupid pony," growled Lottie. "I want to win!" I felt deflated. She clearly hadn't learnt her lesson after all. The final fence was approaching fast and I only had a few seconds to decide what to do. I couldn't let her win after treating me so badly.

I refused the fence and, as Lottie had already folded forwards into her jumping position, she flew over my head and landed in a heap on the floor. She immediately jumped up and, before even brushing herself off, stormed towards me.

"I can't believe you did that!" she shouted. "I hate you, you're the worst pony in the world!" As she reached me she grabbed my reins and gave them a sharp tug. Quick as a flash, Becky appeared beside us.

"This is your very last warning, Lottie. You need to think hard about your behaviour. I'll be having a word with your mum to discuss continuing your lessons here." Lottie burst into tears, apologising to Becky and giving me a cuddle.

Lesson learnt

Becky did speak to Lottie's mum, who was horrified at her behaviour. They agreed that Lottie should help with the yard chores for two weeks as punishment for treating me so badly.

Ever since that day she's changed for the better – although Mitzy is still a bit distrustful of her. She always has a polo in her pocket for me and she's become a lot kinder, which has really improved her riding. Plus, we now know how to deal with any riders who don't treat us well, so remember it always pays to be kind to your fave riding school ponies!

Make A PAPER PONY PAL

Make yourself a super-cute pony pal for your desk or bedside table. Here's how

You'll need...

- two different coloured sheets of card
- scissors
- glue
- googly eyes
- pencil
- pen

Ta-dah!

TOP TIP
Why not use some contrasting coloured card to give your pony some markings?

How to make them

TURN TO PAGE 101 FOR THE TEMPLATES

1. Trace and cut out the templates, then draw around them on a sheet of card.

2. Cut out the front and back of the pony.

3. Stick googly eyes and any paper face markings onto your pony's face. Use a pen to draw his nostrils.

TOP TIP

To turn your pony into a unicorn – draw and cut out a small triangle, then glue it between his ears.

4. Using the second sheet of card, create a forelock and tail and stick them on.

5. To make the body, measure out two coloured strips 3x25cm, one in each colour. Glue the two strips together at one end to create a right angle.

6. Fold the bottom strip over the top strip, then fold the other strip back over the top. Keep folding until you reach the end of the strips and glue the ends together to form the body.

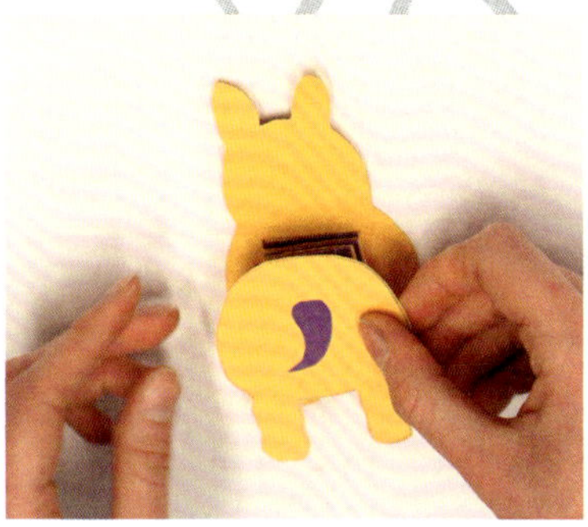

7. Glue the body between the two front and back pieces, and stand him up. You've created your pony pal!

FUN

QUIZ
Are you READY TO GO PRO?

Reckon you've got what it takes to ride alongside the professionals? Take the quiz to find out

1. When going cross-country, you'll be wearing your hat and body protector, but what other piece of kit will you need?

- Your lucky bracelet
- A schooling whip
- Funky cross-country colours

2. When out hacking, which of these is the most important?

- Staying safe and enjoying the ride
- Messing about and having a laugh with your friends
- Trotting for the whole ride to help get your pony super-fit

3. You really need to work on some flatwork before a Pony Club rally. Do you...

- Take your pony for a hack with your friends – it'll help boost his fitness
- Practise in the arena – boring but effective!
- Go for a jump – dressage can wait until tomorrow

4. **When getting your pony ready for a schooling session, do you...**

- Tack him up without grooming – he's been in his stable, so isn't very muddy
- Give him loads of cuddles and a very brief groom
- Give him a quick groom, making sure you pick out his feet, and detangle his mane and tail

5. **At a showjumping competition, what should you do when you enter the ring?**

- Trot around the arena and wait for the judge's bell
- Stand in the middle – there's no point wasting your pony's energy before you start!
- Show your pony all the jumps – you shouldn't start until he's seen every filler

6. **When you arrive at the yard, what do you do first?**

- Find your best friends – it's time to have a catch-up
- Check your pony's happy, and has enough food and water
- Start mucking out and have a general clean-up

7. **When getting ready for a competition, what's the last thing you load into the lorry?**

- Your pony – he doesn't want to be waiting around for anything
- Your kit – you might remember something at the last minute
- Your lunch box – going hungry would be a disaster!

8. **At a dressage comp, what kit should you be wearing?**

- Coloured jodhpurs and a coat or jumper
- Whatever you want – anything goes!
- White jodhpurs with a shirt, tie and jacket

9. **It's time to prep for your lesson. How do you get ready?**

- Tack your pony up and you're ready to go!
- Groom, tack up and head to the arena early so you have time to warm up before your instructor arrives
- Tack up, then brush the bits that are still showing while waiting for your instructor

Turn to page 100 to find out your results.

10. **At a show, when there's a long wait in-between your classes, what do you do?**

- Stay on board your pony – you want to see how all your friends do
- Keep riding in the collecting ring so you're ready for the next class
- Take your pony back to the trailer and make sure he's happily tied up with water and a haynet

COLLECT UP YOUR *marks*

Collectives are the four marks at the bottom of every dressage test sheet. But what do they mean?

In dressage tests, not only are you judged on the movements you ride, but also on the collectives at the bottom of your test sheet. These include your pony's paces, impulsion and submission, and your riding. Each collective is marked out of 10 and doubled, so they have a big influence on your overall score.

They can seem confusing, but once they're broken down they make sense. Plus, there's loads you can work on when you're schooling to boost your collective scores – it'll improve your pony's skills, too, even if you don't compete!

SCORING SYSTEMS

You'll be given a mark from 0–10 for the collectives, and half marks can be given, too. The scores have the following meaning...

- 10 Excellent
- 9 Very good
- 8 Good
- 7 Fairly good
- 6 Satisfactory
- 5 Sufficient
- 4 Insufficient
- 3 Fairly bad
- 2 Bad
- 1 Very bad
- 0 Not executed

DID YOU KNOW?

If two riders tie on the same score in a dressage test, the collective marks are looked at. The combination with the higher collective marks is placed above the one with lower collective marks.

PACES

Jargon... freedom and regularity

Busted! This is all about how your pony moves. The judge will be looking for even, rhythmical paces without being lazy or rushing. When he's moving correctly, he should be tracking up, which means his hind hooves land in the same place as his front hoofprints.

How to improve it... The best way to boost this collective mark is to make sure your pony's paces are active and cover the ground. You can do this by...

- **using polework** Trot and canter poles are a fab way to improve his rhythm, as they encourage your pony to take the same size stride every time
- **counting out loud** It might sound silly, but counting as you ride helps you notice if your pony's speeding up or slowing down, which will help you maintain a consistent rhythm ➤

TOP TIP
Remember to ride any exercises on both reins to keep your pony balanced.

IMPULSION

Jargon... desire to move forwards, elasticity of the steps, suppleness of the back and engagement of the hindquarters

Busted! Impulsion is your pony's energy. He should be pushing through from his hindquarters, rather than leaning on your hands. This is linked to his paces – improve his impulsion and it'll improve how he moves, too.

How to improve it... Remember that impulsion isn't the same as speed. Your pony's energy comes from your legs, but it's important to keep an even rein contact to maintain it. Think of your pony as a toothpaste tube – you want to squeeze with your legs to push enough toothpaste out, but your hands are the lid that stop too much coming out in one go!

Try out these tips to get your pony's impulsion up to scratch...

- **transitions** These keep your pony responsive to your aids and forward off your leg. Try riding transitions at every other marker in the arena. When you can do that well, try every marker!
- **spiral circles** To help engage his hindquarters and keep him supple, you can use spiral circles in trot. Start on a 20m circle, then use your leg to make the circle smaller. When you reach 10m, push him back out again.
- **hillwork** Riding up hills is a fab way to engage his hindquarters and really get him to push himself forward. Start in walk before moving into trot and canter, where the ground conditions allow. It'll help improve his fitness, too!

"Improve his impulsion and it'll improve how he moves, too"

SUBMISSION

Jargon... attention and confidence, harmony, lightness and ease of the movements, acceptance of the bridle and lightness of the forehand

Busted! Submission is how your pony accepts your aids. He should be quick to respond without resisting. Head tossing, tail swishing and being above or below the bit are all signs that he's resisting.

How to improve it... You can tell when your pony's accepting his bit and bridle because he'll feel light in your hands. You'll be able to focus on his way of going and your position, instead of feeling like he's going to pull you down and out of the saddle. Work on it by...

- **riding plenty of shapes** Circles, changes of rein, teardrops and serpentines all keep his mind active and help keep him soft.
- **softening your hands** The most common cause of resistance is too much rein contact, as this can be uncomfortable for your pony. Keep your hands soft with an elastic contact. Think of it like holding a toddler's hand – you want to make sure they can't run away, but don't hold on too tight or you'll hurt them!
- **riding transitions** These help keep him soft and light in your hand, while still responding to your leg aids.

TOP TIP
Using arena mirrors is another great way to check out your position!

RIDER POSITION

Jargon... Position and seat of the rider, correct use of the aids

Busted! This is all about how effective and correct you are as a rider. As well as focusing on your position in the saddle, the judge will be looking at how you ask your pony to do things, such as riding transitions and shapes.

How to improve it... Practice makes perfect when it comes to your position and you'll find that the more experience you have in the saddle, the more this mark will improve. Ways you can work on it include...

- **having a lunge lesson** This gives you the chance to focus on your position without having to worry about what you're asking your pony to do, as your instructor's in control. It'll feel weird at first, but you'll soon get used to it!
- **ask a friend to watch you schooling** This helps you iron out any bad habits, even when you're not having a lesson – they can give you a friendly reminder when your position slips!
- **video yourself riding** This allows you to look back on how you were riding and see what areas you need to do extra work on.

HORSE SPORTS

POLO

Are you a speed demon with a competitive streak? If so, you may have what it takes to become a polo pro!

DID YOU KNOW?
Polo was an Olympic sport from 1900 to 1936.

Polo's a super-fun sport that's a bit like hockey on horseback. It requires speed and stamina, and you've also got to be able to accelerate, stop and turn quickly. So, the stronger the bond and communication between you and your pony, the better!

What is it?

Polo's a team sport with four players on each side. The game is played by swinging a stick to hit the ball and scoring through your opponent's goal. The stick is usually made from bamboo cane with a head of hard wood, but plastic alternatives are becoming more and more common.

A match is split into four, six or eight seven-minute sections called chukkas. The players change their ponies in-between chukkas to make sure they stay super-speedy. Polo is played on a perfectly flat grass field that's bigger than the size of seven football pitches.

Player positions

Each of the four players has a job to do...

- No.1 is the goal scorer
- No.2 can do every job, from scoring goals to heading off their opponents
- No.3 makes sure the ball goes to the correct player
- No.4 defends and protects the goal from the other team

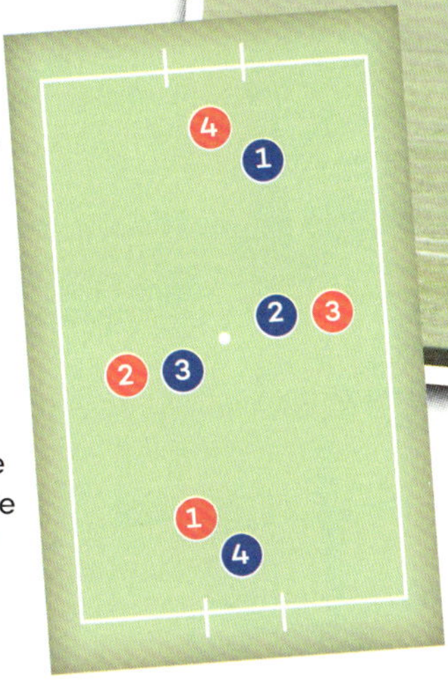

Unlike many other team games, there are no boundaries that mark where each player is allowed to ride – anyone can go anywhere!

Each registered player is given a handicap, which helps to rank them during competitions. This is between -2 (beginner) and 10 (super-pro), with the team rating calculated by adding together the four players' handicaps.

Playing by the rules

There are two umpires on horseback to make sure the rules are followed. The most common foul is when a player crosses the line of the ball. This is the imaginary line the ball is travelling on – the pony closest to the line has the right of way. Riders are not allowed to cross over the line of play and must pass each other right side to right side.

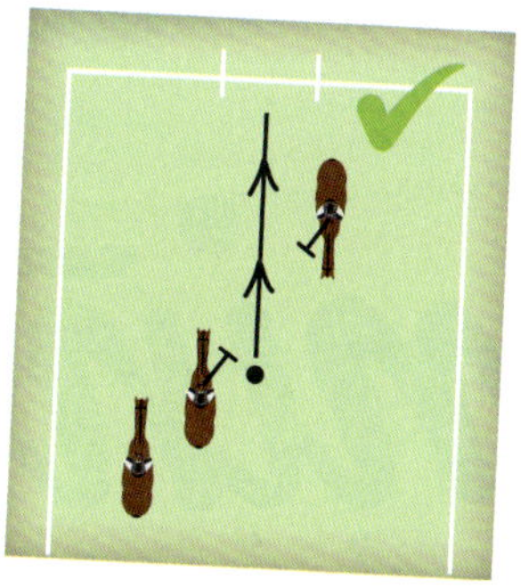

DID YOU KNOW?
Argentina is considered the global capital of polo because they hold the top team ranking and have won five world championships!

Useful lingo

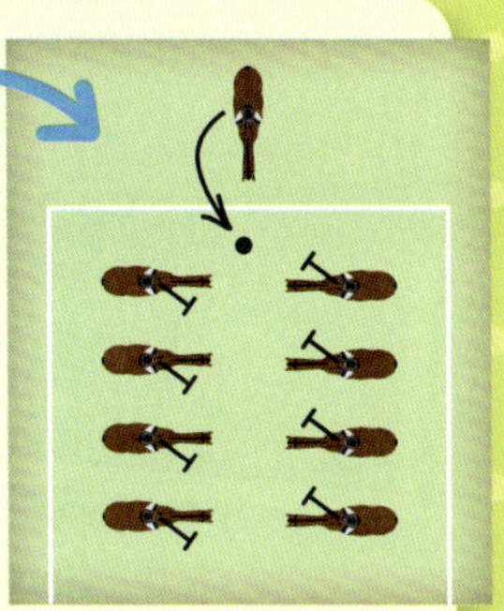

Throw-in When the umpire throws the ball in-between the team line ups to start or resume play.
Ends The two halves of the field – the teams swap every time a goal is scored.
Intervals The three-minute rest period between chukkas – used to switch ponies.
Out-of-bounds When the ball goes off the pitch, it's out-of-bounds and must then be thrown back into play.
Polo ponies Although normally called ponies, the most common height in pro teams is 15–16hh.
Puttees Supportive leg wraps worn by ponies to protect them from injury.
Ride-off When a player tries to win priority over the ball by safely riding sideways into their opposition.
Treading-in At half time, the crowd helps to keep the field flat by treading down all the turf that's been kicked up.

Get involved!

Many Pony Club branches and centres offer polo as an activity. If your branch or centre doesn't have a team yet, why not speak to your instructor and set one up with a group of friends and their speedy ponies?

There are also two Pony Club competition badges up for grabs! The Intro to Polo badge covers the basics, while the Polo badge outlines the rules to help you become a more successful player.

DID YOU KNOW?
Cross-country day at Badminton can draw crowds of up to 250,000 people!

Badminton HORSE TRIALS

Your need-to-know guide to the world's most famous three-day event

Badminton Horse Trials is one of only six top-level three-day events in the world, known as four-stars. An event for the biggest names and the very best in the business, Badminton runs over five days every May and there's loads for spectators to enjoy. Here's everything you need to know...

History

Taking place in Gloucestershire, in the beautiful grounds of Badminton House, Badminton Horse Trials was first held in 1949 by the 10th Duke of Beaufort to allow British riders to train for the Olympics. Although it was originally intended for British competitors, it quickly became known across the world as one of the very best competitions. Now, it also makes up part of the prestigious Rolex Grand Slam of Eventing – to claim it, riders must win Badminton, Burghley and Kentucky consecutively. Only two riders have managed it in 20 years!

Anneli Drummond-Hay wins in 1962

Biggest and best

If one thing's for certain, it's that four-star events are no walk in the park. Riders compete in dressage, cross-country and showjumping over three days and are awarded penalty points for each phase. The horse and rider with the lowest overall score at the end is the winner, so there's no room for mistakes.

Once the tricky manoeuvres of the dressage phase are out of the way, riders and their mounts face a long and gruelling cross-country course with around 45 different fences the next day. These fences have a maximum height of 1.20m, but can be super-wide, too! The final 1.30m showjumping phase is make or break, as the difference between winning or dropping out of the top placings could be knocking down just one pole or finishing a few seconds behind the time!

Tim Price is one of the celeb riders you can spot at Badminton!

Nicola Wilson and Annie Clover

DID YOU KNOW?
In 2011, Sir Mark Todd became the oldest rider to win Badminton at 55.

Badminton highlights

If you're heading to Badminton, make sure you make the most of it with an action-packed, horse-mad day!

☆ **Go for the dressage** It might not be the most dramatic of phases, but there's loads you can learn watching top riders strut their stuff and it'll really make you appreciate flatwork! Head to the collecting ring for some serious celeb-spotting.

☆ **Walk the cross-country course** Getting up-close and personal with the whopping fences is definitely something you won't want to miss. It's a great way to see all the different types of challenge the competitors will face, too.

☆ **Bring your pocket money** There are loads of horsey tradestands where you'll be able to pick up some awesome stuff for you and your fave pony!

DID YOU KNOW?
Andrew Nicholson has completed Badminton 37 times – more than any other rider!

Penalties

Knowing how many penalties are awarded for each section can be confusing – here's what it all means...

CROSS-COUNTRY

First refusal at a fence **20 penalties**
Second refusal at a fence **40 penalties**
Third refusal on the course **Elimination**
Horse or rider fall **Elimination**
Each second over the time limit **0.4 penalties**

SHOWJUMPING

First refusal **Four penalties**
Second refusal **Elimination**
Knocking down a fence **Four penalties**
Each second over the time limit **One penalty**

Rescue Misson

When Frankie went for a quiet hack with her pony, she never expected it to turn into such an adventure

It had been a really hot few weeks, which made it difficult to ride. I didn't want my pony, Nellie, getting too hot because she hated it, so to beat the hot weather I decided I'd get up super-early and go for a hack while it was still cool. I let my mum know what I'd planned and where we were going, set my alarm and went to bed.

The next morning I woke up feeling a bit groggy, got dressed and slipped out the back door. Nellie was surprised to see me so early, but happily tucked in to her breakfast while I busied myself getting her tack and grooming kit together. Once she'd finished eating, I took her out of her stable and gave her a thorough groom before tacking her up.

"I hope you're ready, Nells," I chatted to her as I put her saddle on. "We're going to the common and those sandy tracks will be empty – perfect for a gallop!" Her ears pricked at the word gallop, she definitely knew what that meant.

We're really lucky living right in the middle of the South Downs National Park because we have some great hacking and don't have to ride on the roads at all. We started off at a gentle trot so Nellie was well warmed up before we hit the gallop tracks. The morning was perfect – cool and sunny, and there was no one around except us. We had a blast, racing up the tracks as fast as we could. We'd been riding for an hour and the sun was starting to feel a bit warm, so we turned for home.

Something in the bushes

We ambled along and I let Nellie have her head so she could cool off and stretch. I was enjoying listening to the birds when I noticed a mewing sound joining in.

"That's odd," I thought, "what would a cat be doing all the way out here?" I began to look around, but couldn't see anything. Suddenly, Nellie stopped and snorted loudly. Just ahead of us a small ginger kitten appeared from underneath the brambles.

I immediately jumped off Nellie and passed her reins over her head so I could reach down to the kitten. I stretched out my hand for her to sniff.

"It's all right little one," I coaxed. "If you let me pick you up, I can get you some help." She was very pretty with striking yellow eyes and a white belly and paws. She was very small and looked like she'd been on her own for a while. She crept towards me and, very slowly and carefully, I picked her up. She was so frail I could feel some of her ribs.

Luckily, as there was a bit of a chill when I first went out, I'd put on a light jacket. It had deep pockets – just the right size for a small kitten. I put her in my pocket and remounted Nellie, making sure I didn't disturb the kitten too much.

"Okay, Nellie, let's get her home," I said as I picked up my reins and squeezed her forward. I rode as fast and carefully as I could, desperately trying not to jostle the kitten in my pocket.

> "Suddenly, Nellie stopped and snorted loudly"

To the rescue

When we arrived home, I quickly put Nellie in her field and rushed into the house.

"Mum, we need to go to the vets!" I shouted as soon as I got in the door. "Frankie, what's wrong?!" she exclaimed, running into the kitchen still in her pyjamas. "Has something happened to Nellie? Are you both okay?" I started to explain as I carefully removed the kitten from my pocket. "We're fine, but on our hack we found this tiny kitten. I don't think she's very old and she's really skinny. She needs help fast."

"Right, wrap her in a towel and get in the car, I'll get changed and we'll drive her over to the vets," she said already rushing back upstairs.

Soon we were zooming down the country lanes to our local vets, the kitten cocooned in the towel.

"I called ahead, so they know we're coming. I can't believe she was all alone," Mum said. "Hopefully we'll be able to find her owner." I nodded and didn't say anything. I hadn't thought about the kitten having an owner – I wanted to keep her.

We pulled up at the vets and rushed into the reception area.

"Hi, I called earlier, we have the young kitten," Mum said striding up to the reception desk. The girl behind the desk stood up: "Follow me to the examination room, Dr Harlow is waiting for you all." We followed her down the hallway and into one of the rooms.

"Dr Harlow, this is the family with the kitten" the receptionist explained. "Is that her in the towel? Pop her up here on the table so I can take a look." I carefully put the kitten and towel on the table and held my breath while the vet examined her.

"Hmmm, she's not in a good way," Dr Harlow said after the longest two minutes of my life. "She's covered in fleas and is very malnourished. She's only around three weeks old and shouldn't be away from her mother yet. We'll keep her in for observation, but be warned she might not make it."

"We'll leave her in your capable hands," Mum said, ushering me out of the room. "Please call us as soon as you have an update. We'd like to know if the owners can be found, too." I couldn't believe we were just leaving her. I felt numb thinking that she might not be okay, I might have found her too late.

A long wait

I was quiet the entire drive home and went straight out to find Nellie.

"I don't know if she's going to be okay Nell, she's so ill!" I sobbed into her neck. Nellie continued to munch on some grass, but I already felt comforted by her presence. Deciding that the best way to get through the day was distraction, I caught Nellie and spent my time giving her a bath and pamper session as well as doing some tidying up on the yard. It was nearly dark when Mum finally called me in for supper and I reluctantly headed back inside.

"Frankie, before you ask, I've not heard anything from the vets," Mum said before I'd taken off my boots. "I'll ring in the morning for an update." I nodded, ate my dinner, then went upstairs to bed. I was so worried about the poor kitten that I struggled to fall asleep.

The next morning, I woke up early and rushed downstairs to find Mum. She was already up and talking on the phone. I waited impatiently for her to finish.

"Well?!" I asked as soon as she ended the call. "She's going to be okay!" Mum said beaming. "Dr Harlow said she's doing really well and if no owners have come forward by the end of the day I've agreed to foster her for the time being." I couldn't believe my ears. "Really?" I squealed. Mum was still smiling as she replied: "If no one comes forward we can keep her, but once she's well and big enough she can live outside on the yard with Nellie and help keep the feed room mouse-free. What do you think?"

"This is the best news ever!" I was thrilled. "I think we should call her Tiger, she's the same colour and has to be fierce to survive all she's been through."

A home for life

We brought Tiger home the next day. She still wasn't back to full strength, so we had to nurse her at home for a few weeks. She grew really quickly and as no one came forward to claim her, she stayed with us. Now, she and Nellie are inseparable. Tiger often follows us on our hacks or sits and watches us while we practise our jumping. Now I'm always on the look out for other unexpected animals while out hacking.

QUIZ

Are you a GROOMING GURU?

Do you know everything there is to know about grooming? Test your knowledge by helping Jasmine get Monty ready

1. Jasmine's not got a lot of time before her lesson, but Monty's come in from the field covered in mud. What should she do?

- **A** Give him a full groom now – she'll just have to be late for her lesson
- **B** Quickly groom the areas where his tack will sit – she can give him a proper groom after her lesson
- **C** Tack him up without grooming him – she doesn't want to be too late

2. What equipment does Jasmine need to pick out Monty's feet?

- **A** She doesn't need anything, she can use her fingers
- **B** A hoof pick and skip
- **C** Just a hoof pick

3. Monty's mane is starting to look a little long and Jasmine decides she wants to smarten him up. When's the best time to pull his mane?

- **A** While Monty's warm after the lesson because his pores will be open, making his mane easier to pull
- **B** It doesn't really matter when she does it, just whenever she's got time
- **C** Just before her next ride so he looks super-smart

4. **Next Jasmine decides to use a dandy brush. What should she use it for?**

A To brush out his tail

B For grooming Monty's face

C For removing mud and dirt from Monty's body and legs

5. **How many times a day should Jasmine pick out Monty's feet?**

A One

B Two

C Three

6. **Next, Jasmine takes a metal curry comb from her grooming kit. What does she use it for?**

A To clean the grease and scurf from her body brush

B To help Monty get rid of his winter coat

C To comb Monty's mane and tail

7. **Roughly how long should it take Jasmine to give Monty a full groom?**

A Two hours

B One hour

C 40 minutes

8. **What's the piece of grooming kit is in this picture?**

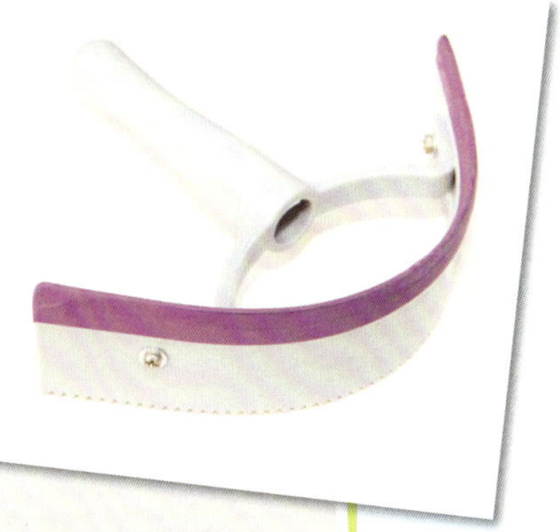

A Shedding tool

B Curry comb

C Sweat scraper

9. **Next, Jasmine needs to detangle Monty's mane and tail. What shouldn't she use?**

A A plastic curry comb

B Her fingers

C A mane and tail brush

10. **To finish, a friend suggests Jasmine uses a stable rubber, but what is it?**

A It's a special eraser that will remove any black marks from Monty's coat

B It's a piece of cloth used to clean the walls of Monty's stable so he doesn't get dirty

C It's a piece of cloth that's folded into a small square and Jasmine should use it to add shine to Monty's coat

Turn to page 100 to find out how you got on!

DID YOU KNOW?
The Boomerang Trophy is named after showjumper Eddie Macken's horse. The pair won the Derby four years in a row from 1976–1979!

THE *Hickstead* DERBY

It's one of showjumping's toughest tests and takes place at a world-famous course. Here's everything you need to know

The Hickstead Derby is one of the UK's most prestigious competitions and it was first run in 1961 at the famous All England Jumping Course in West Sussex. The world's top showjumpers compete every June for the chance to take home the winning title and Boomerang Trophy, one of the most sought-after prizes in showjumping.

What's a Derby?

Derbies take place outside in a grass arena and combine classic showjumping fences with some that might look more familiar on a cross-country course. Derby courses are typically much longer than those found in regular showjumping and the Hickstead Derby course has 23 jumping efforts.

History

The All England Jumping Course was built in 1960 – the year before the first Derby – by a man called Douglas Bunn, whose dream was to create an impressive showground in England to rival those in Europe. Since then, some of the biggest names in showjumping have lifted the Hickstead trophy, including Ben Maher, Nick Skelton and Tina Fletcher, and there have only been 56 clear rounds.

Best of both

In showjumping, you'd normally expect to try to maintain an even canter all the way around the course, but because of the varied terrain and very different fences, riders find themselves having to change their horse's canter to suit the upcoming fence. If you're approaching a very wide water jump, it's not a great idea to approach in a short, springy canter unless you want to get wet!

Fence factfiles

DID YOU KNOW?
The first woman to win the Hickstead Derby was Marion Coakes. She won in 1967 on Stroller, a 14.1hh pony, when she was just 20 years old – amazing!

PRIVET HEDGE

Height: 1.50m
Width: 1.98m
This super-wide oxer has been known to catch a few horses out, with some trying to treat it like a bank and landing on top of it!

DEVIL'S DYKE

Height: 1.42–1.44m
This triple-whammy can be tricky for horses to see due to the uneven ground and the fact that the rails are all the same colour. It has a bright blue ditch under the middle fence, which really ups the spook-factor!

THE BANK

Height: 3.20m
This is without doubt the course's most famous and toughest test! With a huge climb, a metre-high rail at the top, followed by a very steep drop and two strides to a whopping 1.60m rail, the bank is not an obstacle for the faint-hearted.

Showjumping SUCCESS!

Make this year your most successful one yet by ensuring your showjumping competition goes as smoothly as possible

Showjumping can be fast and furious, with riders battling it out over fences to keep the poles up and finish in the fastest time. With the smallest thing making the difference between getting your hands on a red rosette and missing out, it's vital your day runs smoothly so you can bring your A game to the ring.

TOP TIP

If it's your first show, it's a good idea to enter a clear round class. They're a great way to get a feel for the atmosphere and see how your pony will react to being somewhere new without the added pressure of competing!

TOP TIP

You should always keep an eye on your pony's shoes, but check them extra-carefully in the run-up to a show. You don't want to get there to find out he has a loose shoe and you can't compete!

Sort the schedule

There's plenty to think about before you even get to the show! First, you'll need to have a look at the schedule to work out what classes you want to enter. It's always best to compete at a lower level or height than you're practising at home to make sure you and your pony are confident on the day. Check whether you'll need to enter in advance or if they're taking entries on the day.

Pre-show prep

Make the most of the day before the show to get yourself organised. You'll need to...

- give your pony a thorough groom or, if the weather's warm enough, a bath. It's polite to look clean and presentable at a competition, so even if you can't do a full-body bath, be sure to remove any stable stains

- take your tack apart and give it a proper clean – that includes under all the buckles, too! As well as getting it shiny and spotless, it's a great time to check the stitching for any weaknesses
- clean his boots (and yours!), if he wears them, and make sure you've got a clean saddle pad on his saddle
- find all the things you'll need to take with you and load any non-valuable items into the car or lorry the day before

TOP TIP

Wake up in plenty of time on the morning of your competition – there's nothing worse than rushing round and worrying about being late!

The big day

When you arrive at the show, head to the secretary's office to pick up your number. Most showjumping classes have a board by the collecting ring with a list of rider numbers – this is the order they'll call you in to jump. It's a good idea to head there next to find out what time your class will be running and to put your number down on the board.

TOP TIP

When you're walking the course, use markers such as trees or fence posts as a visual guide so you know where to turn to meet the fence well.

TOP TIP

It can be useful to watch a couple of other competitors ride the course – as well as helping you remember which way to go, it can give you a useful insight into how it's riding, which parts are tricky and the best lines to take.

Walk it off

Your course walk is one of the most important things you can do to make sure your round goes well! It's not only the best way to learn which order to jump the fences in, but it lets you plan the lines you'll ride, too. This is vital to give you a good approach to every fence, which means you're less likely to have a stop or run-out, or knock any poles down.

Most showjumping competitions are two phase, which means there will be a second, timed part of the course. You normally jump this straightaway if you go clear in the first section, so make sure you walk this part, too!

Collecting ring chaos

The collecting ring is where you warm up for your class and it can be a super-busy place. There are some unwritten rules you need to follow to make sure you and everyone else in the ring stays safe. Make sure you...

- **pass left-to-left** This means that when passing an oncoming rider, you pass with them on your left-hand-side. So if you're on the right rein, you'll need to move to the inside track unless you're in a faster pace, in which case you take priority on the outside
- **avoid riding across the take-off and landing area of the warm-up fences** This is really dangerous as it could cause a collision or refusal if someone else is jumping
- **call which fence you're jumping as you approach it** This lets everyone know who's jumping what. Remember to leave plenty of space between ponies, just in case the pony in front knocks a rail or has a refusal.

- **check the gateway's clear before entering and leaving the ring** Always check that no-one's about to ride across the entrance before you go in or out of the ring
- **keep an eye on the other riders at all times** Always check behind you before making a downwards transition – try to find your own space first. It's also bad manners to ask for canter when you're right next to another pony, as it could cause them to become overexcited

The call-up

When it's your turn to jump and you've entered the ring, don't forget to wait for the buzzer before you start! This shows that the judges are ready – jump the first fence before the buzzer and you'll be eliminated.

You have 45 seconds once the buzzer has sounded to cross the start line. It's a good idea to practise this at home because it's longer than you think. Take the time to create a canter with plenty of impulsion, so you approach the first fence well.

Over the finish line

Remember, you haven't completed the course until you've crossed the finish line, so don't stop riding when you land from the final fence. Once you're through, leave the arena promptly so the next rider can start their round.

"Don't forget to wait for the buzzer before you start!"

TOP TIP

Even if you hear your pony clip a pole while you're jumping, never look back at the previous fence to check if it's still up! It's super-tempting, but it'll affect your line and approach to the next fence, which could result in another knock-down.

Remember these tips and you'll find your big competition day runs without a hitch – now go out there and win some rosettes!

Fabulous FELLS

These striking natives are hardy and hardworking, but do you know everything about Fells?

Native BREEDS

Fell ponies have long been popular as both riding and driving ponies. They're easily recognisable with their flowing manes and tails, glossy coats and long feather. They're a hardy breed and well-adapted to the rugged terrain of the north west of England.

Way back when

Fell ponies have been around for a long time, and were used by both the Vikings and Romans for farm and ridden work. Friesian horses brought over from Europe by the Roman armies are thought to have had an impact on the breed and Fells are often mistakenly called mini Friesians.

Their strength, size, fast walk and trot made them ideal for use as pack ponies, and they would travel up and down the country transporting goods in pack trains. These trains would often travel from The Lake District to London, which is more than 250 miles! They were also popular as pit ponies and were used both above ground and down in the mines to move coal well into the 20th Century.

During the Victorian era, the ponies became increasingly popular as trotting ponies for racing. Races were regularly held and competitors would trot their ponies through a course around their village. These races often drew large crowds that would turn out to see their favourite pony compete.

DID YOU KNOW?

You can still find ponies roaming on the Fells, however, they're not truly wild because they have an owner who looks after them.

DID YOU KNOW?
Queen Elizabeth II is a fan of the Fell pony and is regularly seen riding them through Windsor Great Park.

The modern breed

The Polo and Riding pony stud book saw the first Fell ponies registered in 1898, but it wasn't until the establishment of the Fell Pony Society in 1922 that the Fell Pony stud book was created. The stud was set up to help protect and improve the breed.

Although you may be familiar with Fell ponies having a glossy black coat, this wasn't always the case. When the Fell Pony Society was first formed, bay and brown ponies were very common colours with a few grey ponies registered, too.

DID YOU KNOW?
Due to their great temperament and steady gait, Fell ponies are a popular choice with the Riding for the Disabled Association.

Fact file

Height: No bigger than 14hh
Colour: Black, brown, bay and grey
Place of origin: Cumbria
Known for: Fast walk and ground-covering trot

What do they do now?

These ponies are great all-rounders and can be ridden by adults or children. They're still famed for their striking looks, great temperaments and for being sure-footed. This makes them a popular choice for hunting and they're often shown as working hunter ponies.

Due to their great characters and stamina, they're also used for trekking or endurance. Plus, they're regularly used for both competitive and pleasure driving.

Fell ponies can still be found helping out with farm work, including shepherding, light forestry and helping to transport equipment.

DID YOU KNOW?
Although Fells can have small white markings, more than half the breed have no white markings at all.

QUIZ

Can you do A HEALTH CHECK?

Are you a pony healthcare know-it-all?
Take our quiz to find out!

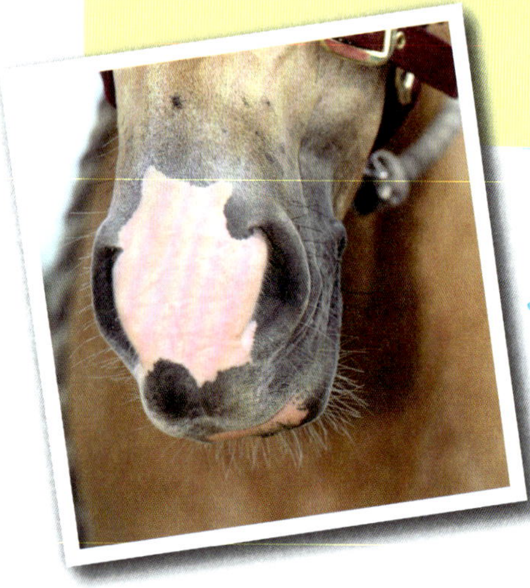

1. **Which of these is NOT a way to check your pony's breathing rate?**

   A Hold your hand near his nostrils to feel each breath

   B Trot him really fast on the lunge so he starts puffing

   C Watch his ribcage, which will expand as he breathes in

2. **What should your pony's temperature be if he's healthy?**

   A 37.2–38.3°C

   B 46.4–48.6°C

   C 62.5–64.8°C

3. **What's the name of the pulse that starts bounding if your pony has laminitis?** (Hint – you'll find it in the body part pictured!)

   A Digital pulse

   B Leg pulse

   C Analog pulse

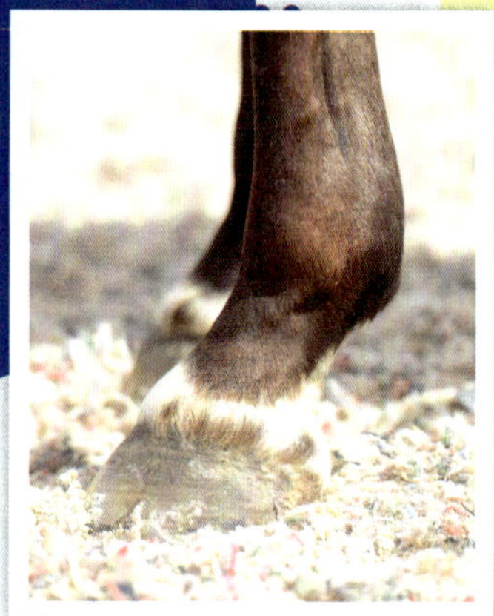

4. **When checking your pony's pulse, it's important that you always use your thumb, rather than your fingers.**

   A True

   B False

5. **When you listen to your fave pony's tummy, you should hear it make lots of different noises.**

   A True

   B False

6. **If your pony's gums are dry or sticky, this could be a sign of which problem?**

   A Cold or flu

   B He's feeling a bit overtired

   C Dehydration

7. **If your pony's healthy, what should his eyes be?**

   A Wide and staring

   B Bright and clear

   C Dull and sleepy

8. **One of your pony's hooves feels warmer than the others. What might cause this?**

   A Thrush

   B He's stepped in fresh poo

   C A hoof abscess

9. **Sweating, rolling, pawing the ground and looking at his tummy are all signs your pony might have what?**

   A Colic

   B Laminitis

   C A headache

10. **Your pony's suddenly started being naughty when you ride him. Why might this be?**

   A He's showing off in front of his friends

   B He just wants to be difficult

   C He's in pain, so ask your vet to check him over

Turn to page 100 to find out how you got on!

Make A PONY HEAT PACK

Stay warm and cosy with this fun pony heat pack

You'll need...

- an old pillowcase
- 60x28cm linen, cotton or fleece fabric
- needle and thread
- scissors
- wool
- coloured felt
- pins
- marker pen
- roughly 500g rice

How to make it...

TOP TIP
Add a few drops of essential oil to the rice to make your heat pack smell lovely when it's warm – try lavender or mint oil.

Make the lining

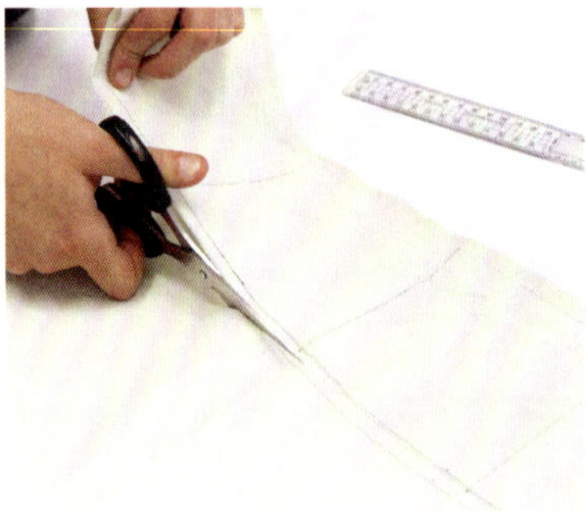

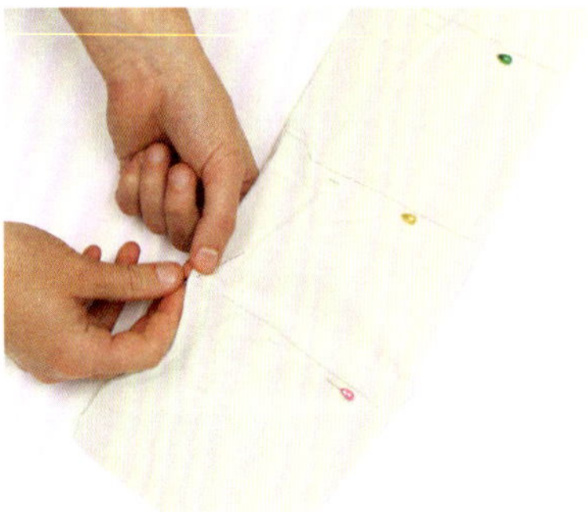

1. Cut the end off an old pillow case, so you've got a pocket of fabric 52x13cm wide.

Ask an adult for help when using scissors and needles.

2. Use a ruler and pencil to divide the pocket into four even sections, then stitch across the pencil lines using back stitch, leaving the long edge of the pillow open. Next, turn it inside-out, making sure you push the corners out.

3. Fill each section of the lining with three tablespoons of rice.

4. Sew up the long edge to close the lining and set it aside.

Make the cover

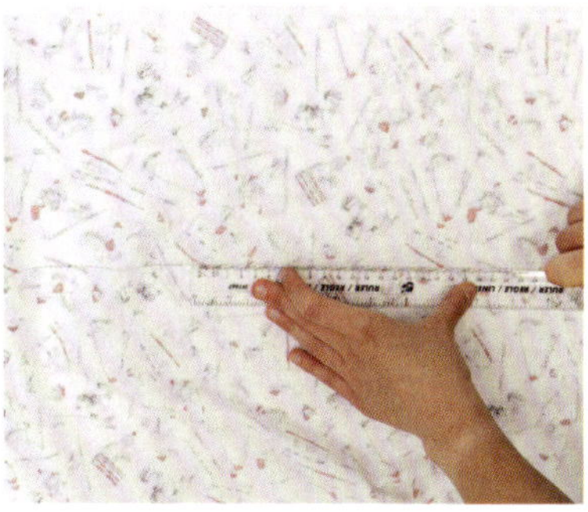

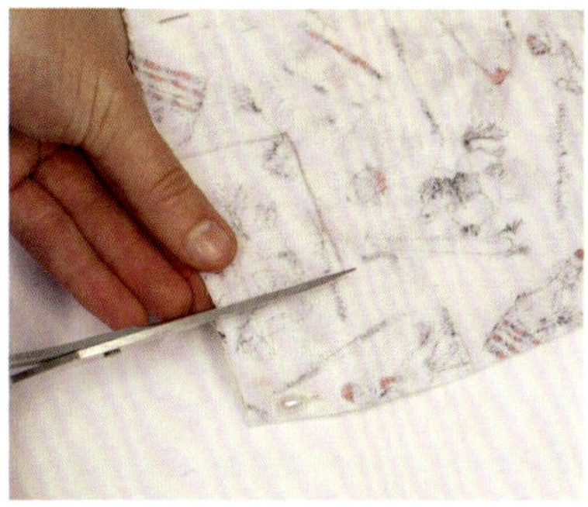

TOP TIP

Visit bit.ly/PONY_SEWING for full instructions on how to master back stitch.

1. Cut out a piece of fabric that's 60x28cm, then fold it in half down the long side, using pins to keep it folded.

2. Draw a 4x4cm square in the middle of each end of the fabric to mark your pony's legs. Cut out the square.

3. Using back stitch, sew around the front and back legs of the pony, and three-quarters of the way up the long side of the body, leaving a large gap to insert the lining. Turn it inside-out, so the stitching is now on the inside. This will form your cover.

TURN TO PAGE 101 FOR THE TEMPLATE

4. Scale up, draw and cut out the template for the pony's head, then draw around it on a piece of felt. Next, cut it out and draw on the pony's features using a marker pen. Stitch it in place near the forelegs.

5. To make the tail, measure out six 20cm strands of wool. Tie them all with one knot in the middle, then using the knot as the top of the tail, sew it in place near the hindlegs. Repeat for the forelock, trimming it to a shorter length.

TOP TIP

You could use an old fleece blanket to create the cover or use fabric that's the same colour as your pony.

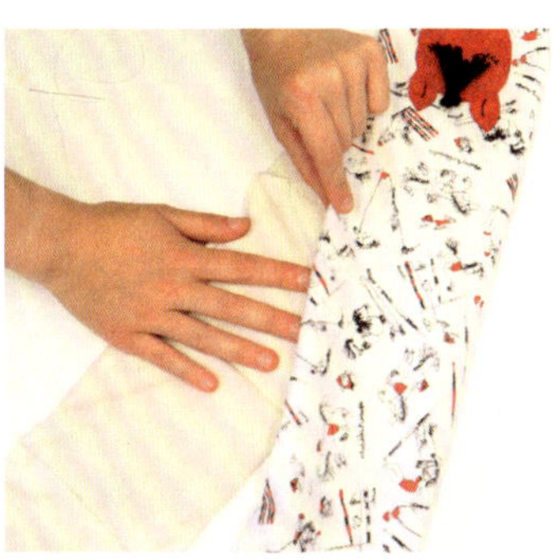

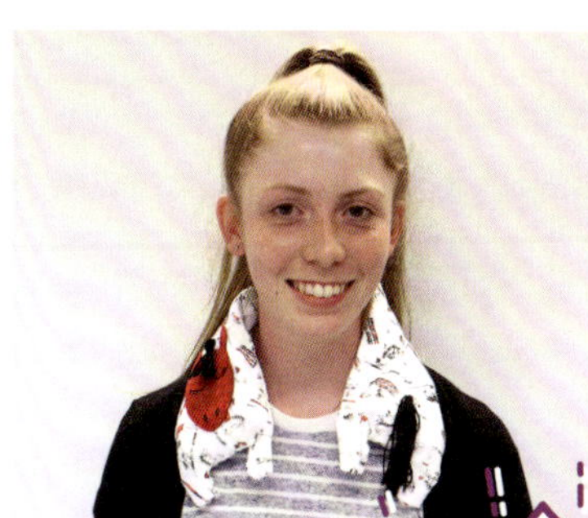

6. Place the lining into the cover, then sew up the gap.

7. Put the heat pack in a clean microwave for 30–60 seconds to warm it up, then place it around your neck. Snuggly!

HORSE SPORTS

HORSEBALL

Ever played netball or rugby? Now imagine playing it on your pony!

DID YOU KNOW?
If the ball's dropped, players aren't allowed to dismount to pick it up. They have to lean over in the saddle and stretch far enough to reach it!

Horseball's often described as a cross between rugby, basketball and polo – and sometimes as quidditch on horseback! But it's definitely not as easy as the pros make it look. Here's everything you need to know!

How is it played?

Horseball requires a ball the size of a small football that's fitted with handles. Two teams of four riders play against each other and the aim is to score goals by throwing the ball through a 1m hoop, which stands 3.5m from the ground at each end of the arena. The team who scores the most goals wins.

Players in a team must pass the ball at least three times in a row before they can score a goal and they can only hold the ball for up to 10 seconds, so they've got to be quick!

The teams don't have long to score those all-important goals, either, as the game is made up of two 10-minute halves, with only three minutes of half time for the players and their ponies to catch their breath.

History

Horseball can be traced back as far as the 1700s to a game in Argentina known as pato. The major difference is that, instead of a ball, players would throw around a live duck in a basket! It even became the country's national sport. Super-weird, right?!

Fast forward to 1970, and a former riding instructor and rugby player in France created a new equestrian game based on pato, and horseball was born. It was brought to the UK in 1991, and now there are clubs up and down the country.

DID YOU KNOW?

There are two referees in every game of horseball, one on foot and one on horseback.

DID YOU KNOW?

Horseball's really popular in France, where there are over 450 clubs!

Who can play horseball?

Well, pretty much anybody! There are three junior categories in British horseball – Poussins (under 11s), Minimes (under 15s) and Cadets (under 17s), as well as a Seniors classification. There are a few clubs in the UK that hold taster sessions – why not find one near you?

What types of ponies can play?

Most horses and ponies are able to play, from tiny Shetland ponies to super-speedy Thoroughbreds! There are pony height restrictions for the different age groups, but any breed can take part.

Lots of horseball players like to retrain ex-racehorses to play the sport because they're clever, pick up new skills quickly and have plenty of stamina. It's also a great opportunity to give horses who are being retired from racing a new home and career.

TOP TIP

If you're having a lesson at a riding school on a pony you haven't ridden before, ask if it's okay to meet him first. Spending some time getting to know him and giving him a groom will make you feel more at ease when you're on board.

CONFIDENCE CLINIC

Are niggling nerves affecting your riding? Here's some great ways to boost your confidence and have fun with your fave pony

Feeling nervous is something that happens to everyone, so don't let it spoil your fun. Whether you're worried about having lessons or getting out and about to shows, there's lots of things you can do to feel more confident and have more fun than ever!

LOVE YOUR LESSONS

Share your worries

Always have a chat with your instructor before you begin your lesson, even if you've had lessons with them before, so you can tell them about your riding experience and what you're hoping to work on. It's important to let them know if you're worried about anything, too, so they can reassure you and help you work on these issues. You'll probably find that once you've told your instructor you're feeling nervous about something, you'll be less worried about doing it!

Turn over for more confidence tips

Don't forget to breathe

You may not even realise you're doing it, but it's very easy to hold your breath when you're feeling nervous, and this can cause you to tense up and tip forward. As well as affecting your position, you'll be letting your pony know you're feeling nervous and that can worry him, too. Instead, try to take long, slow, even breaths. Singing can help keep you breathing, too.

Use a neckstrap

Whether you're riding a new pony or one you know well, it's a really good idea to use a neckstrap. Lots of top riders use them and it's easy to make one out of an old stirrup leather. If you're feeling a bit insecure, or you're about to canter or jump, holding onto the neckstrap will help you stay in balance with your pony.

Fix your fears

You may feel nervous because you're worried about your pony spooking, being strong or refusing a fence, but if you think about it, the best time for something to go wrong is during a lesson! That's because you'll have your instructor there to help you, and they can give you lots of tips and exercises to help fix the issue and reduce the chances of it happening again.

TOP TIP

Some ponies can become unsettled if they're too close to others, which can make you feel nervous, so keep your distance and make sure there's at least one pony's length between you and the pony in front. If you feel you're too close, ride deeper into the corners of the arena or turn a circle, to create more space.

COMPETE WITH CONFIDENCE

Do your homework

Show-day worries are more likely to happen when you're not sure what you have to do, so plan ahead and find out what your class involves. Ask a friend who regularly competes for some tips or ask your instructor for help.

To prepare yourself and your pony you'll need to practise, so if you're entering a jumping class, make sure he's familiar with the different types of fence, and if you're showing or doing dressage, spend time polishing up his flatwork. Having a few lessons in the run-up to the show is a smart idea, too.

TOP TIP

Why not ask your instructor or an experienced adult to come to your next show with you for moral support? They can warm you up, help you walk the course if you're jumping and give you lots of useful feedback at the end of the day.

Don't put yourself under pressure

Everyone wants to do well when they go to a show, but putting yourself under pressure to win will make you even more nervous and you probably won't ride as well as you can. Instead, focus on having fun with your pony and set yourself some clever goals. A great show-day goal would be to ride around a course of showjumps in an even canter rhythm or to ride the roundest circles possible in your dressage test. Doing this will actually improve the way you ride your pony and increase your chances of doing well.

TOP TIP

If you're worried about competing somewhere you've never been before, see if you can hire the venue to school or have a lesson there. Then it'll seem more familiar when you go to the show.

TOP TIP

Go along to a show as a spectator and watch the classes you'd like to enter with your pony. You can learn a lot about what's expected and it'll help you work out what makes a great performance.

> "Focus on having fun with your pony and set yourself some clever goals"

Don't be shy

Lots of riders feel nervous when competing because there are people watching. The best thing to do is forget they're there, and concentrate 100% on your pony and what you need to do in your class. Performing in front of people isn't an easy thing to practise, but you could try schooling when the yard is busier or ask some friends to watch you ride. If you really concentrate on your pony, you'll soon forget they're there.

Remember that no matter who's watching, they'll be willing all of the competitors to do well, so think of them as your own personal fan club rather than an extra set of judges!

Channel your inner Olympian

A really easy way to feel more confident is to use a clever technique called visualisation. What you need to do is imagine yourself clearing a course of fences or riding a perfect canter transition, then when you do a class for real, you're more likely to do well.

You can even pretend you're a famous rider, so next time you turn down the centre line, imagine you're Charlotte Dujardin and see your marks soar!

Life's a picnic

A simple picnic ride turned into a bit of an adventure

Paige and Rio
as **Laura and Bryn**

Katie and Caramac
as **Hattie and Sprout**

Orla and Connor
as **Emily and Dylan**

I think it's this way.
I'm not so sure.
Let's face it, we're completely lost!
Does anyone have any phone signal?
Ponies have a great sense of direction, I'll give Bryn his head.
Not sure, maybe...
Still no signal, do you guys recognise where we are?
I knew you could get us home, Bryn.
I'm sorry I got us lost.
I think we should give the ponies a day off tomorrow.
I really am sorry, next time I'll only suggest paths I know.

I forgot my phone.
My battery died.
Okay, let's head this way and see if I can get some signal.
Me too.
I think I'm starting to recognise where we are.
Is that the yard gate?
That's okay, it was quite an adventure.
Plus, we now know a new route.
I bet they're as tired as us!
Let's not do that again for a while.
Definitely!
The end

Super-smart show ponies

Thrilling showjumping classes

Horse of the Year SHOW

All the insider info on this horsey spectacular

With fantastic classes and dazzling displays, it's no surprise that the Horse of the Year Show (HOYS) is a staple on any equestrian calendar. From Pony Club mounted games to the international showjumping and Puissance classes, this world-class event attracts huge audiences every October.

Prince Philip meeting the mounted games teams

DID YOU KNOW?

The judges decide how high the final Puissance wall will be built. In 1977, legendary showjumper Harvey Smith wasn't happy with sharing first prize with another rider and wanted the wall to get bigger. However, the judges stuck to their guns and finished the class at 7ft 4in.

History

The very first HOYS was held in 1949 in an arena in Harringay, London, after Captain Tony Collings decided there should be a special event to mark the end of the showing season. His aim was to find the champion of champions in the show ring, but it was agreed that showjumping should also be included. And, just like that, HOYS was born!

The first show had an amazing 400 entries and the competition has continued to grow, with its 70th anniversary show hosting 1,600 horses and ponies.

From 1959, the show was held at Wembley Arena in London, but moved to Birmingham's NEC Arena in 2002. HOYS fills a mega 50 acres – that's the equivalent of 252 regular-sized riding arenas!

DID YOU KNOW?
The show is called HOYS because Captain Tony Collings' aim of the event was to find a 'Horse of the Year'.

Hot competition

The Pony Club mounted games creates an electrifying atmosphere, with riders vaulting on and off their ponies at super-high speed. Teams compete throughout the year for a chance to qualify for the finals at HOYS. The five top teams then battle it out for the chance to win the historic Prince Philip Cup.

Higher and higher

The tension and excitement builds throughout the show until the final Saturday evening event – the mighty Puissance. It's a chance to watch top-class showjumpers face the big, red wall and battle it out for the famous title.

Putting on a show

Sticking to its showing roots, HOYS hosts some of the most renowned showing finales of the season. Catering for both little and large, there's an amazing range, from Miniature Horse of the Year to British Ridden Heavy Horse.

Not to be missed...

There's so much to see and do at HOYS, but these should be at the top of your to-do list, including...

DID YOU KNOW?
HOYS showcases over 78 hours of live entertainment each year – that's over three days non-stop!

- ☆ going behind the scenes by visiting the exclusive HOYS Meet the Horses Zone. This is a fab opportunity to say hello to some of the super-cute horsey stars
- ☆ visiting the HOYS Live Zone and rider signing area are also a great way to meet equestrian legends. With daily Q&A sessions, as well as autograph opportunities, it's the perfect entertainment between your fave performances
- ☆ the annual dressage masterclass is hosted by a different pro each year. In 2018, it was the legendary Carl Hester MBE who stepped into the spotlight

Shop til you drop

There's also a huge retail village, which is jam-packed with more than 200 shops and stalls. You're sure to find this season's must-have equestrian items and find a special treat for your fave pony!

QUIZ

WHAT'S INSIDE?

How much do you know about what's going on inside your fave pony? Take this quiz to find out!

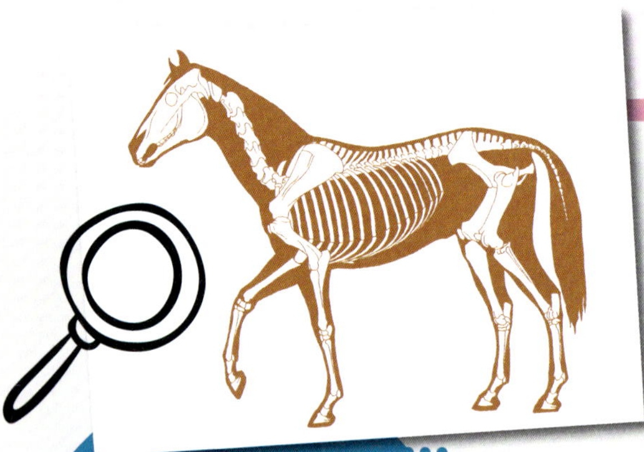

1. **How many bones make up a pony's skeleton?**
   - A 105
   - B 205
   - C 305

2. **An average pony's heart beats around 36 times a minute, but how many times does a racehorse's heart beat each minute when he's galloping?**
   - A 150
   - B 185
   - C 220

3. **What's the total lung capacity of an average horse?**
   - A 25l – about the same as a backpack
   - B 55l – about the same as a holdall
   - C 100l – about the same as a large suitcase

4. **Which of these does a pony not have?**
   - A Collarbone
   - B Tail bones
   - C Cheek bone

5. **From beginning to end, how long would a horse's digestive system be if you laid it out on the ground?**
   - A 4.5m – about the length of a medium-sized car
   - B 20m – about the length of the short side of an arena
   - C 30m – about the length of a netball court

6. **Which type of ball is a similar size to a horse's stomach?**

- **A** Tennis ball
- **B** Rugby ball
- **C** Football

7. **How many teeth does an adult pony have?**

- **A** 20–24
- **B** 28–32
- **C** 36–40

8. **How do ponies' brains compare to adult humans' brains?**

- **A** Horses' brains are smaller
- **B** They are the same size
- **C** Horses' brains are bigger

9. **How many muscles are there in a pony's ear?**

- **A** 4
- **B** 10
- **C** 16

10. **Which part of a pony's body has no muscles?**

- **A** His face
- **B** Between his ribs
- **C** Below his knee and hock

Turn to page 100 to find out how you got on!

Excellent EXMOORS

Exmoor ponies are famous around the world, but how much do you know about the history of this amazing native breed?

Native BREEDS

These hardy, versatile native ponies are the ultimate all-rounders. Exmoor ponies have lived on the moors in Somerset for thousands of years and can still be found grazing the hills today.

DID YOU KNOW?
Exmoor ponies are classified as endangered and are rarer than the Giant Panda!

Early history

Exmoor ponies have been around for thousands of years – during the Iron age they were used to pull chariots. The first written record of the ponies is in the Domesday Book, when Exmoor was designated as a Royal Forest and looked after by a warden.

Historically, the breed was used by farmers as their main form of transport and to hunt and plough the land. When the Royal Forest was sold off in 1818, the ponies were put up for sale, too. The last warden of the Royal Forest bought many of the ponies and his herds became the foundation for the continued existence of the breed – some ponies alive today can trace their bloodlines all the way back to these herds.

Exmoors became increasingly popular as a children's pony in the 1930s after the publication of *Moorland Mousie*, a book narrated by an Exmoor pony.

Exmoors in need

World War II nearly saw the extinction of the Exmoor pony. Many were stolen for their meat by hungry people on rations, some were killed by visiting troops during target practice, while others were lost when people passing through didn't shut gates to the boundaries. By the end of the war, there were thought to be as few as 50 ponies left.

In 1945, the breed was saved by the work of Mary Etherington, who persuaded London Zoo to exhibit two ponies, Caractacus and Foxglove, to highlight the plight of the breed. She also called for the installation of cattle grids to prevent the ponies wandering through open gates.

DID YOU KNOW?

The word pony wasn't used to refer to Exmoor ponies until the mid 1800s. Instead, they were called horsebeasts by the locals.

Modern day ponies

Exmoors are believed to be Britain's oldest breed and modern Exmoor ponies are thought to be relatively unchanged from their ancient ancestors. They still feature some of their original characteristics, including prominent flesh around their eyes to help protect them from bad weather – known as toad eyes.

Today, they're popular as children's ponies as they're extremely adaptable and can turn their hoof to almost anything. Exmoor ponies can often be seen strutting their stuff in the show ring or competing in driving classes.

They also play an important role in conservation grazing, and Exmoor ponies can be found grazing free in Yorkshire and Sussex, as well as in the Exmoor National Park.

Fact file

Height: 11.2–13.2hh
Colour: Bay, brown or dun
Place of origin: Exmoor, Somerset
Known for: Strength, versatility, adaptability and love of food!

DID YOU KNOW?

There are now roughly 3,000 Exmoor ponies worldwide.

TOP 20 Hacking GOALS

Love to explore and go on an adventure? Here's a bucket list of rides to give you some inspo!

1 Picnic ride

When the sun's shining, pack a mega picnic to share with your yard friends so you can have a whole day of hacking fun.

2 Take on a treasure hunt

Ask an adult to plan a route and plant clues along the way. Then get a group of friends together and see if you can complete the trail. You could split into teams to make it competitive.

3 Hit the beach

Nothing beats a long gallop along the shoreline on your fave pony. Plenty of beaches allow you to ride at certain times of the day, so check the schedule and plan a trip. You can organise beach rides through nearby riding centres, too, if you don't have your own pony.

TOP TIP
Always take a fully charged mobile phone with you on a hack in case of emergency.

4 Jump along the way

Jumping on a hack is super-exciting and a great way to get in some extra cross-country practice. Keep an eye out for inviting logs to have some fun with!

5 Horseback safari

What could be better than getting up close and personal with amazing African wildlife? Persuade your parents to take you on hols so you can enjoy galloping alongside wild animals and spotting the African Big Five!

6 Join a sponsored ride

A sponsored ride involves miles of pre-planned hacking with cross-country jumps along the way. Get a group of friends together, start raising some money and have fun while you're at it!

7 Bright and early

Get up first thing for an early morning hack with your fave pony. With the sun rising and birds chirping, it'll be bliss!

8 New Forest adventure

Why not take your pony exploring somewhere totally new like the New Forest? There's plenty of wildlife and you may even spot some mares with their foals.

9

Mountain climbing

Enjoy some stunning views while navigating tricky terrain. Hills are also great for your pony's fitness, which is an added bonus!

10

Hacking holiday

You'll have the chance to explore exciting new places and riding a different pony can really help improve your riding, too.

11

Let it snow!

Riding in the snow is magical – wait for a white-out and ride in a winter wonderland.

12

Get swimming

Best done in a warm country with an experienced guide, there's nothing more exciting than riding on the back of a swimming pony.

13

Iceland trekking

Not only is it super-fun to ride a new pony – especially an Icelandic with special paces – you'll get to explore the awesome landscape, too.

14 Group gathering

Get a group of your best mates together and plan a fun trek on your ponies.

15 A famous affair

Ever fancied riding round Badminton or Burghley? Enter the sponsored rides held each year after the world-famous competitions. It'll give you the chance to explore the beautiful estate and see the massive fences up close!

16 Ride among royalty

Windsor Great Park has miles of gorgeous hacking and, if you're lucky, you might even spot the Queen out and about on one of her Fell ponies!

DON'T FORGET!
Make sure you and your pony are both kitted out in high-vis.

17 Make a splash

Get your pony's feet wet by hacking through a river. It's great for helping him cool off on a hot day and a good chance to practise for cross-country, too!

18 National Park exploring

There are loads of beautiful national parks you can ride in all over the country, so get researching!

19 Wild west

Ever dreamed of being a cowgirl or boy? A ranching holiday will give you a true western experience, with activities such as rounding up cattle and barrel racing.

20 Epic endurance

Plan your own route on a map, pack a bag with plenty of water and a few snacks, then head off for a day exploring your local area.

PONY PARADISE

Create the perfect environment to keep your pony entertained

As a special treat, why not combine all your pony's fave veggie treats into one **hanging snack**? Popular options include turnip, swede, parsnip, carrot and apple.

Split his hay into **two smaller nets**, one on each side of his stable, to encourage him to move around more. Plus, liven them up by hiding some carrot and parsnip in them.

Float some apples in your pony's water bucket to make a DIY **apple bobbing challenge**. The fruity additions will provide him with loads of entertainment and encourage him to drink more, too!

Treat balls are a great way to keep your pony active and amused. By filling the toy with some of his favourite nibbles, he'll enjoy working for the prize.

Another scrummy option is a **hanging treat** such as a lick or forage ball. They're available in loads of different flavours, and some even contain essential vits and mins. Hanging treats are difficult to nibble and will keep him busy for hours.

Does your pony love a scratch? Stable **scratch pads** are a fab way for him to enjoy the benefits of a good groom any time. Plus, it won't damage his mane and tail like rubbing on the door does!

TOP TIP

Sugar-free treats are the best option to keep your fave pony's diet healthy.

DID YOU KNOW?

If your pony's bored in his stable, he's more likely to become stressed and develop bad habits called stereotypies.

DID YOU KNOW?

Even if he's kept really entertained, it's still super-important that your pony's checked regularly throughout the day.

WIN A PONY BED FOR YOUR ROOM!
PONY
THE UK'S NO1 PONY MAGAZINE
PONYMAG.COM
TEST YOUR JUMPING SKILLS
LOVE
MANAGING PODGY PONIES
HARNESS THE POWER OF POSITIVE THINKING
XC RIDE LIKE A PRO
MAKE tasty PONY TREATS
QUIZ! WHAT DISCIPLINE SHOULD YOU TRY?
COOL SUMMER TOPS!
WIN A MEGA COMPETITION OUTFIT
MEGA PONY CLUB MAGAZINE INSIDE
PONY meets WILLIAM FOX-PITT
JUMPING STRONG PONIES SORTED
MAKE YOUR PONY sparkle
HOW TO IMPRESS YOUR YARD OWNER
FUN HACKING QUIZ
WIN A COOL SUMMER WARDROBE!
ALL ABOUT YOUR PONY'S TEETH
RIDE A JUMP OFF LIKE A WHITAKER
FUN XC QUIZ
PONY Chat
WIN
awesome prizes every issue in the magazine and online
See yourself in PONY
SHOUT OUT!
MY PONY CLUB
SUPER-CUTE PETS
WIN A SUMMER WARDROBE FROM MOUNTAIN HORSE!
One lucky reader will win a stylish clothing collection!
QUESTION WHAT ARE THE GLOVES CALLED?
PLUS
cute posters, fun quizzes, cringeworthy horsey fess-ups, real-life dramas and loads more!
Join the PONY community at ponymag.com and on...
YouTube
facebook.com/ponymag
@ponymaguk
ON SALE EVERY 4 WEEKS AT ALL GOOD NEWSAGENTS AND SUPERMARKETS

Make PERSONALISED PONY KIT

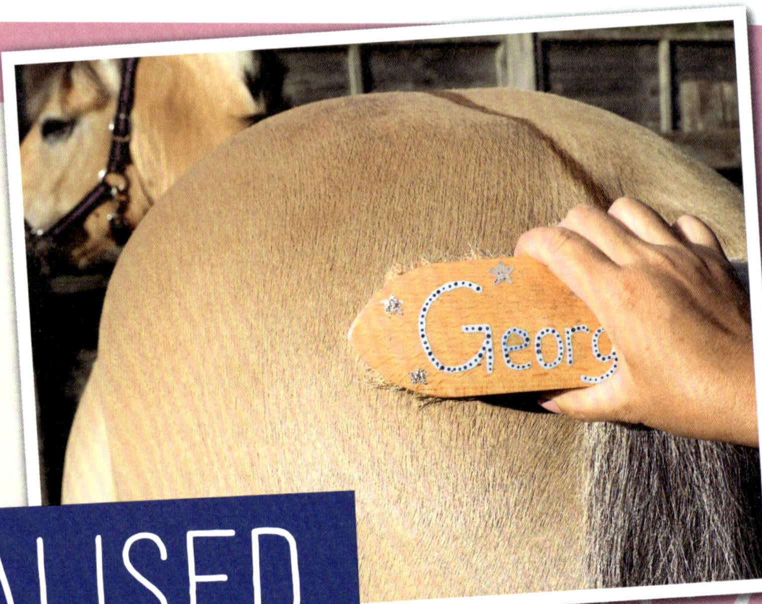

Make your buckets and brushes unique to you and your fave pony!

You'll need...

- ✓ grooming brush
- ✓ enamel paint
- ✓ glitter (optional)
- ✓ paintbrush

TOP TIP
For an extra-tough seal, varnish your brush when the paint's dry.

How to do it...

Brushes

1. Take any stickers off your brush – you might need to soak it to remove any really stubborn or sticky bits.

2. Plan your design on paper.

3. Using enamel paint and glitter, decorate your brush. Then leave it to dry.

You'll need...

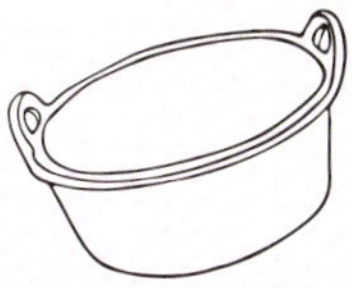

- plain feed bucket
- water-resistant outdoor spray paint
- card
- pencil
- sticky tape
- scissors

TOP TIP
Keep your designs simple.

Buckets

1. Draw a stencil of your pony's name and any designs you'd like to use onto card – we used an empty cereal box.

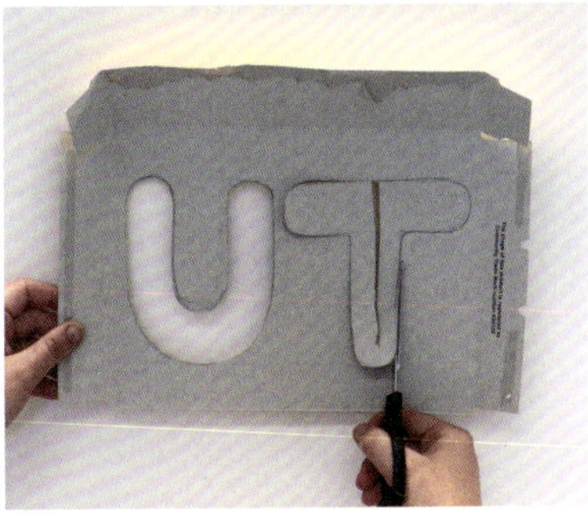

2. Cut out your stencils and take your bowl outside.

TOP TIP
Spray the paint slowly to minimise drips.

3. Tape your name stencil onto your bowl and cover the rest up with newspaper.

4. Spray the paint from a safe distance.

Check the directions on the can and ask an adult to help you.

5. Take off the name stencil and use the design stencil to decorate the rest of your bucket.

Superb SUFFOLK PUNCHES

These gentle giants used to be a regular sight on farms, but how much do you know about them?

The breed has long been a popular choice for farm work due to their cleverness and hard-working attitude. These gorgeous chesnut horses used to be a regular sight on farmland throughout the UK, but with modern farming machinery taking their jobs, they're now an endangered breed.

DID YOU KNOW?
Suffolk Punches are the UK's oldest breed of heavy horse.

DID YOU KNOW?
Traditionally, the word chestnut is spelt 'chesnut' without the 't' when referring to Suffolk Punches.

DID YOU KNOW?
Suffolk Punches are often referred to as Suffolks or Suffolk Horses.

Early history

Suffolks were extremely popular during the 1800s as they were the tractors of their day and were used for ploughing as well as pulling heavy loads. They were also used to help build railways in London by moving heavy equipment.

The Suffolk Horse Society was formed in 1877 to help promote the welfare of the breed and it actively encouraged farmers to breed from their horses.

They gained popularity as war horses during the Boer and Crimea wars because they were well-known for their reliability and ability to work hard in difficult conditions. Suffolks were also recruited in World War I to pull ambulances, supplies and ammunition.

World domination

During the early 20th century, Suffolks also gained popularity abroad, with horses being exported all over the world to countries such as America, Australia and Japan!

DID YOU KNOW?
Twenty-nine Suffolk Punch foals were born during 2017.

Fact file

Height: 15.3–17hh
Colour: Chesnut, which is categorised into liver, dark, red, light or bright. They can have some white markings on their face and legs, and flecks in their coat
Place of origin: East Anglia
Known for: Strength, power and endurance

Decline of the breed

After World War II, Suffolk Punches saw a drastic decline, as tractors became a popular choice for agricultural work. In 1966, just 11 foals were born and it was feared that the breed could become extinct. The Suffolk Horse Society took steps to help ensure the future of the breed, including giving grants to breeders and owners.

Modern day Suffolk Punch

Nowadays, Suffolk Punches are still used in agriculture, especially for conservation work, but they're also gaining in popularity as riding horses and can be seen in the show ring or at ploughing matches. Every year, the Suffolk Spectacular show celebrates everything Suffolk, including Suffolk Punches.

HIT THE ROAD

Make sure your pony's ready to travel by stocking up on the essentials

When travelling your pony, whether it's just around the corner or across the country, its super-important that he's fully kitted out with everything he needs for the journey. It's just as important to make sure you've got the right safety gear on when you load him, too. Here's what you need to get on the road...

Wear a **riding hat** while loading and unloading your pony in case he accidentally knocks into you.

Using a **tail guard or bandage** will protect his tail from being rubbed.

A **leather or safety headcollar and leadrope** is essential for keeping your pony safe and secure while you're on the move.

Travel boots give your pony's legs protection against knocks or scrapes while loading and travelling.

Gloves protect you from rope burn if your pony pulls away while you're loading. Make sure you have **sturdy footwear**, too, to avoid squashed toes.

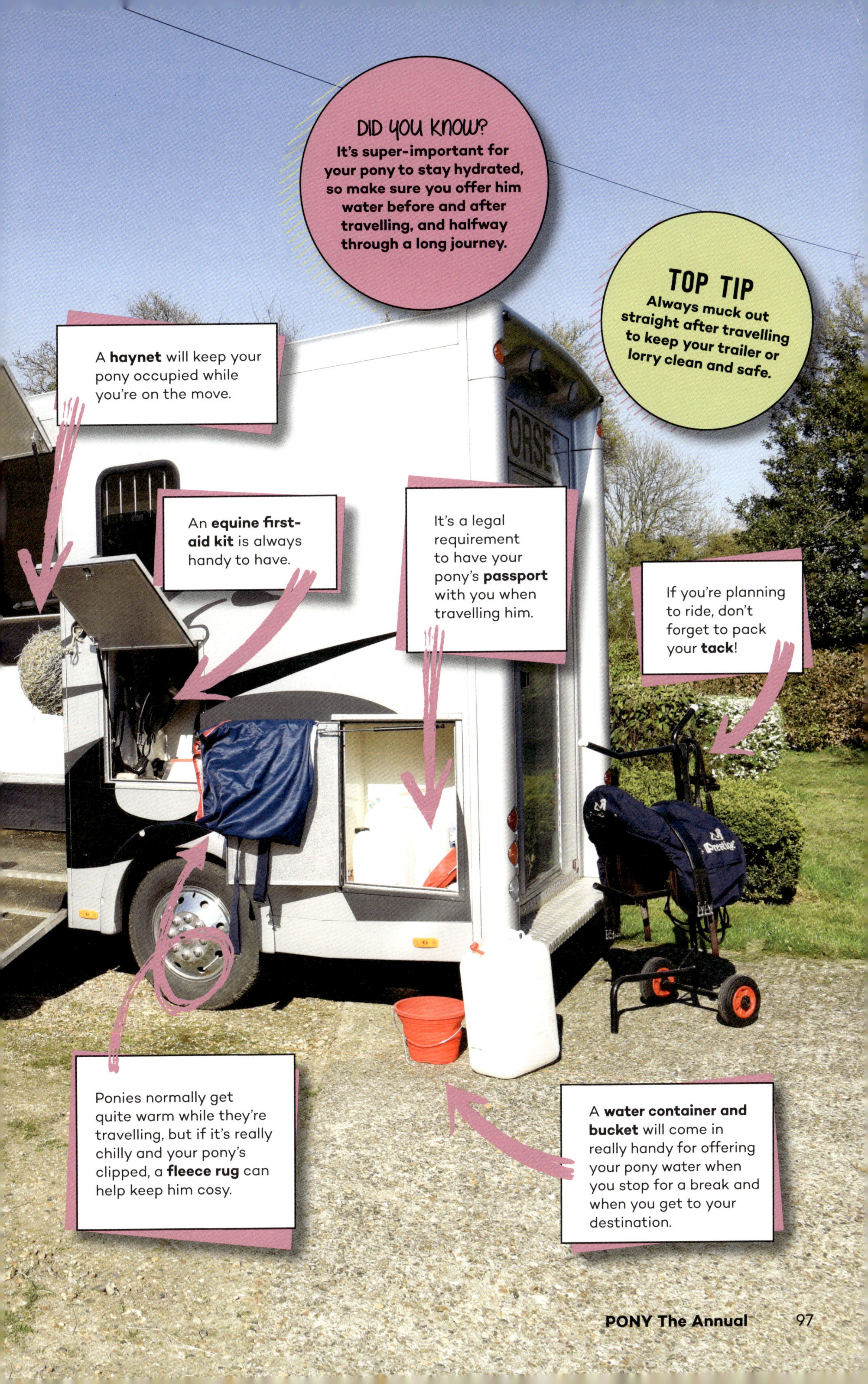

DID YOU KNOW?

It's super-important for your pony to stay hydrated, so make sure you offer him water before and after travelling, and halfway through a long journey.

TOP TIP

Always muck out straight after travelling to keep your trailer or lorry clean and safe.

A **haynet** will keep your pony occupied while you're on the move.

An **equine first-aid kit** is always handy to have.

It's a legal requirement to have your pony's **passport** with you when travelling him.

If you're planning to ride, don't forget to pack your **tack**!

Ponies normally get quite warm while they're travelling, but if it's really chilly and your pony's clipped, a **fleece rug** can help keep him cosy.

A **water container and bucket** will come in really handy for offering your pony water when you stop for a break and when you get to your destination.

Back in time

Ellie would never have guessed that a holiday in the Irish mountains could be so magical

Ellie was bored. Her parents had promised that a holiday to Ireland would be fun, but so far all it had done was rain. They were staying in a cabin in the mountains and there was no signal, so she couldn't even text her friends. They'd been there three days, but it felt like a million years to Ellie and they still had a week of holiday left. How was she ever going to survive that long?

Ellie was staring out of the window at the drab grey scenery when she thought she saw a flash of white. She stared harder through the glass of the window. There it was again – it looked like a pony!

"There's a pony outside, I think it's in trouble. I'm going to see!" she called to her parents as she raced out of the door. "No, Ellie, wait!" came her mum's muffled reply as the door slammed shut behind her.

Ellie ran down the hill to where she thought she'd seen the pony, but nothing was there. Feeling disappointed, she began to trudge back up to the cabin when the bush next to her began to rustle. Carefully, she peered through the leaves and saw the same flash of white coat she'd seen earlier.

"I was right," she thought, "he must be so cold and hungry." She crept as quietly as she could around the bush, so as not to startle the pony, and she couldn't believe her eyes. It wasn't a pony at all, but a silver unicorn.

Unbelievable

He was a gorgeous silver white that shimmered slightly, even in the murkiness of the day, and he had golden hooves and a huge, shiny golden horn set in-between his kind brown eyes. Ellie pinched herself to check she hadn't dozed off in the cabin and started dreaming. When she didn't wake up she had to believe he was real.

He moved suddenly, startling her. Ellie jumped backwards, steadied herself and had another look at the unicorn in front of her. She noticed that his back leg had become caught in some old fencing that had fallen and he couldn't free himself.

Very slowly and carefully, Ellie moved towards the fencing to have a closer look.

"Okay, I think I'll be able to lift this off you," she said softly to the unicorn. "I'll do my best, but it might hurt a little." He kept still and blinked slowly at her, and Ellie decided he understood. She took a deep breath, counted to three and tried to lift the fence. She strained and strained, but couldn't lift it far. With a huge effort, she managed to lift it just enough for the unicorn to free himself.

> "Ellie pinched herself to check she hadn't dozed off"

Magical new friends

With a huff she let go of the fence, expecting the unicorn to be long gone. To her surprise, he stood watching her intently and took a tentative step towards her. She stretched out her hand and, after a quick sniff, he walked closer until she could stroke his soft neck. He nickered gently and there was a small popping sound, and they both stepped back from each other.

"Oh, thank you!" said a small voice from somewhere near Ellie's ear. She whirled round, trying to find the source of the voice, but she couldn't see anyone.

"You didn't just speak did you?!" Ellie asked the unicorn. He gave a snort that sounded suspiciously like a laugh and shook his head. "It was me, silly girl!" said the voice, accompanied by a sharp tug on Ellie's hair. "Ouch!" Ellie exclaimed, turning her head to peer at her left shoulder, on which sat what she could only describe as a fairy. The fairy was beautiful, with pale pink skin, blue hair and delicate, green shimmery wings that extended past her head.

"Thank you for saving Topaz. I don't know how we'd have helped him on our own," the fairy gushed.

"My name's Rain, what's yours?" Ellie replied: "I'm Ellie, you're a fairy aren't you?" Rain smiled, "Yes, I'm a Unicorn Keeper fairy. Unicorns don't usually show themselves to humans because they get hunted for wishes and the healing powers of their hair. However, you saw Topaz because while he was panicking about being stuck, I left to get help and wasn't shielding him. I don't have any kinetic magic so couldn't shift the fence off him."

"What magic do you have? Can Topaz talk? Are any of the myths about unicorns true?" Ellie had a million questions whizzing round her brain – she couldn't wait to tell her friends she'd met a unicorn and a fairy.

"Well, some myths are true. They're magic and do exist – obviously. I think we could show you better than we could tell you," Rain mused. "Topaz can't talk but as well as having gifts of wish-granting and healing, he has the power of time. He can show you the past and how unicorns came to be. My magic is more simple, I can create illusions." With that, Rain turned and pointed to Topaz who now resembled a bay pony. "Wow! Can you show me anything else?"

"Yes, anywhere you want to go. Consider it a gift for helping Topaz. I should warn you, though, you won't be able to talk about anything you learn today because the magic protecting the unicorns prevents anyone who's seen one from talking about it," warned Rain.

Where it all began

"Please show me how unicorns came to be," asked a very excited Ellie. "Okay, but you've got to promise to do exactly as I say," Rain looked at her sternly. When Ellie nodded vigorously, she continued. "Topaz will kneel down, and you'll get on and hold onto his mane. Then you'll need to shut your eyes as we travel through time, because it can make you feel quite ill. When we get there, you've got to stay on board Topaz. Ready?"

Topaz knelt down on the ground and looked expectantly at Ellie. She ran over to him and scrambled up onto his back, wrapped her hand in his mane and shut her eyes tight. "I'm ready," she said to Rain. Ellie suddenly felt like she was being squeezed by a huge elastic band and was worried she might be sick, but it was soon over.

"You can open your eyes again now," came Rain's soft voice. Ellie opened her eyes and gasped. All traces of the cabin had gone. There was only the rugged countryside of the Irish mountains stretching to the coast.

"Watch the beach carefully," whispered Rain. As Ellie looked, she could see the crests of the waves begin to get bigger and bigger. The larger they got, the more they began to look like horses and ponies. Then, one of the waves didn't crash onto the sand but instead continued to gallop onto the beach and others soon followed until there were hundreds of silver unicorns.

"That's amazing, I've never seen anything so beautiful!" gasped Ellie. "It's stunning," replied Rain. "Now you know how unicorns were born and why they're silver and gold. The silver is from the glistening waves and the gold is the sunlight that gets trapped in the water." They stood watching for a few more minutes, then Topaz gave a warning whinny.

"I'm sorry Ellie, but the magic won't let us stay any longer," Rain said sadly. "We've got to go back, close your eyes."

Back to reality

After another uncomfortable journey, they were back on the soggy mountainside next to the cabin. Ellie gently slid of Topaz's back and gave him a quick hug.

"Thank you both for such an amazing time, this has been the best afternoon of my life!" She started to turn away but Rain spoke. "We'd like to give you this unicorn hair bracelet as a token of thanks. It's very rare and its magical healing properties will make sure you never become ill." Rain smiled as she handed Ellie a beautiful bracelet woven out of hair with fine gold beads as decoration. "I'll never forget you. Will I ever get to see you again?" asked Ellie. "You might see us again or any other magical creatures. The bracelet marks you as a unicorn friend, so others might reveal themselves to you. Now go or your parents will worry."

Ellie turned, ran back up towards the cabin and, as she got to the door, turned to wave to Rain and Topaz, but they'd already gone. She made her way back inside and stood quietly while her mum scolded her for running out in the rain without a coat, all the while gripping the bracelet in her pocket tightly before slipping it onto her wrist.

The rest of her holiday sped by in a blur. The rain finally let up, and Ellie and her family spent their time exploring the countryside. Although Ellie didn't see anymore unicorns, she thought she'd caught a glimpse of some fairies while walking with her parents. Next time you're out exploring the countryside, keep your eyes peeled – you never know what you might find.

THE ANSWERS

Page 42 ARE YOU READY TO GO PRO?

Mostly riding hats
Congrats, you're definitely ready to go pro! You know exactly how to handle competitions, so it's time to get out and about, and hopefully take home some red rosettes!

Mostly carrots
Well done, you may not be quite ready to make it as a top rider, but you're well on your way. Keep improving by reading all the fab PONY mag articles and you'll soon be out competing with the pros. Hard work pays off!

Mostly horseshoes
Oh dear, it looks like you have some work to do before you're ready to become a pony pro. Why not offer to help groom for a friend at a competition? It'll be a great experience and will help you prepare for your next competition.

Page 54 ARE YOU A GROOMING GURU?

1 B, **2** B, **3** A, **4** C, **5** B, **6** A, **7** C, **8** C, **9** A, **10** C

0-4 correct answers
It looks like you need to brush up on your grooming know-how, but with some practice you'll have it nailed in no time. There are loads of books that can help you, and check out PONY mag for fab grooming tips.

5-8 correct answers
You've clearly been working hard to improve your knowledge and you know your mane comb from your curry comb, but there's still a little way to go.

9-10 correct answers
When people have a grooming-related question, you're the person they always ask. Your pony's known for being the cleanest on the yard and you're often found spending the day with a brush in your hand, giving him a perfect pamper sesh!

Page 64 CAN YOU DO A HEALTH CHECK?

1 B
2 A
3 A
4 B. False – you should use your index or middle finger, as your thumb has its own pulse.
5 A. True – not hearing any sounds could mean there's a problem with your pony's digestive system, such as colic.
6 C
7 B
8 C
9 A
10 C

1-4 correct answers
Oh no! You've got a little way to go before you're confident at spotting the signs of pony health, but don't worry, it's a tricky subject and there's loads of ways to boost your knowledge. You'll get there soon enough.

5-7 correct answers
You know lots of the signs to look out for, but there's still room for improvement. Keep an eye on the features in PONY mag to help you brush up on your skills, and you'll be a pony health guru in no time.

8-10 correct answers
Wow, maybe you should consider a career as a vet! You can always spot when something's not quite right with your pony and all your yard mates ask you for advice. Keep up the good work!

Page 80 WHAT'S INSIDE?

1 B, **2** C, **3** B, **4** A, **5** C, **6** B, **7** C, **8** A, **9** C, **10** C

Make TEMPLATES

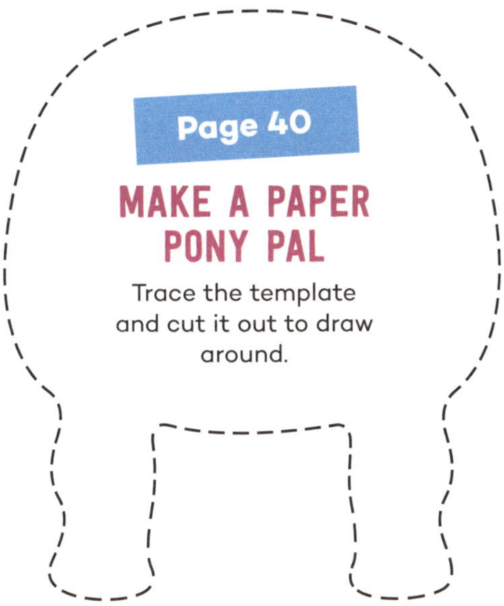

Page 40

MAKE A PAPER PONY PAL

Trace the template and cut it out to draw around.

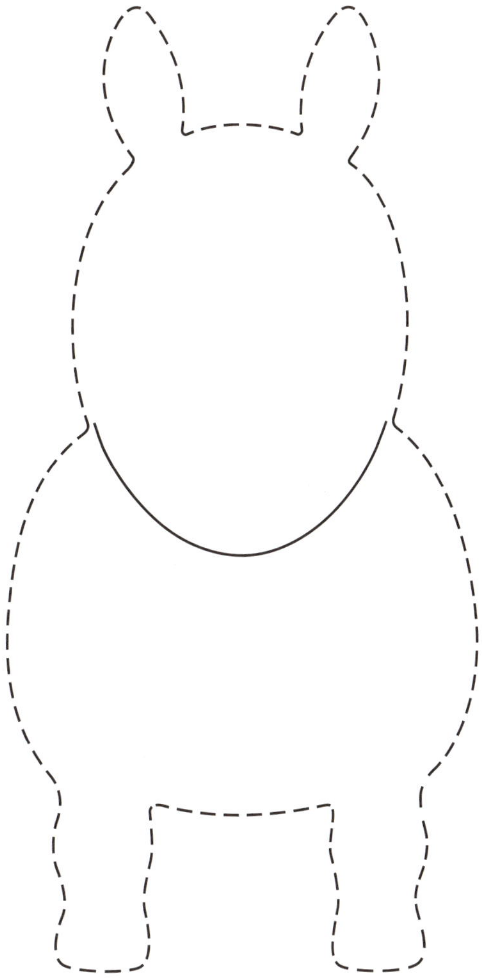

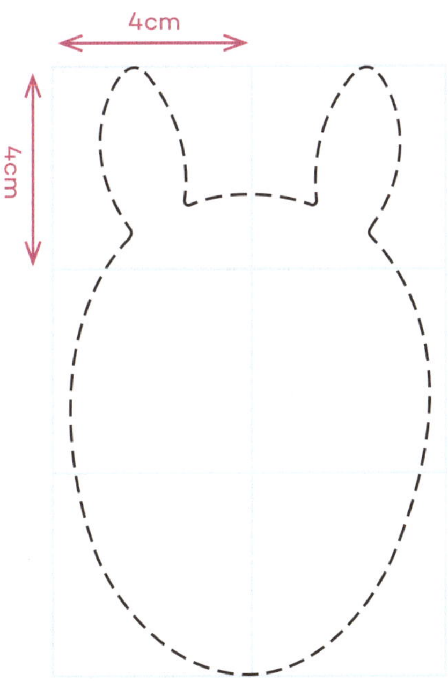

Page 66

MAKE A PONY HEAT PACK

Draw the grid to size on an A4 piece of paper and copy the shape.

Photography Bob Atkins **Cover photo** Bob Atkins **Pages 6–7** Kit Houghton/Olympia Horse Show **Pages 16–17** MoD Crown, Peter Nixon for Royal Windsor Horse Show **Pages 18–19** 1st Class Images **Pages 30–31** Hickstead, Jeremy Colwill **Pages 48–49** Michael Chevis **Pages 50–51** Kit Houghton/Mitsubishi Motors Badminton Horse Trials **Pages 56–57** Hickstead **Pages 68–69** DrewsViews Photography, Horse-Ball M3, Su Scott **Pages 78–79** 1st Class Images, E.S Photography, Real Time Imaging, RTI **Pages 102–103** Illustrations by Helena Öhmark and Rebecca Öhmark

THE MISADVENTURES OF CHARLIE!